THE GODFATHER LOVER'S GUIDE TO
SICILY

To the Sicilians and their unparalleled hospitality
And for the film aficionados turned travellers.

THE GODFATHER LOVER'S GUIDE TO
SICILY

KAREN M. SPENCE

WHITE OWL
AN IMPRINT OF PEN & SWORD BOOKS LTD.
YORKSHIRE – PHILADELPHIA

First published in Great Britain in 2025 by
White Owl
An imprint of
Pen & Sword Books Ltd.
Yorkshire – Philadelphia

Copyright © Karen M. Spence, 2025

ISBN 978 1 03611 659 0

The right of Karen M. Spence to be identified as author of this work has been asserted by her in accordance with the Copyright, Designs and Patents Act 1988.

A CIP catalogue record for this book is available from the British Library.

All rights reserved. No part of this book may be reproduced or transmitted in any form or by any means, electronic or mechanical including photocopying, recording or by any information storage and retrieval system, without permission from the Publisher in writing.

Printed and bound in India by Replika Press Pvt. Ltd.
Design: SJmagic DESIGN SERVICES, India.

Pen & Sword Books Ltd. incorporates the imprints of Pen & Sword Books: After the Battle, Archaeology, Atlas, Aviation, Battleground, Discovery, Family History, History, Maritime, Military, Politics, Select, Transport, True Crime, Fiction, Frontline Books, Leo Cooper, Praetorian Press, Seaforth Publishing, Wharncliffe and White Owl.

For a complete list of Pen & Sword titles please contact

PEN & SWORD BOOKS LIMITED
George House, Beevor Street, Off Pontefract Road, Hoyle Mill, Barnsley, South Yorkshire, England, S71 1HN.
E-mail: enquiries@pen-and-sword.co.uk
Website: www.pen-and-sword.co.uk

or

PEN AND SWORD BOOKS
1950 Lawrence Rd, Havertown, PA 19083, USA
E-mail: uspen-and-sword@casematepublishers.com
Website: www.penandswordbooks.com

CONTENTS

INTRODUCTION..6

CHAPTER 1
***THE GODFATHER*: A DIFFICULT BIRTH**.............8

CHAPTER 2
SAVOCA...15

CHAPTER 3
FORZA D'AGRÒ...38

CHAPTER 4
MOTTA CAMASTRA..65

CHAPTER 5
TAORMINA AND SURROUNDS..........................76

CHAPTER 6
ACIREALE AND SURROUNDS...........................96

CHAPTER 7
PALERMO AND SURROUNDS..........................116

CHAPTER 8
MAINLAND ITALY...136

CHAPTER 9
CORLEONE, SICILY..157

ACKNOWLEDGEMENTS.....................................166

BIBLIOGRAPHY..167

INDEX..178

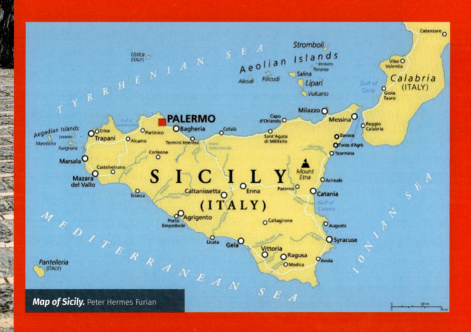

Map of Sicily. Peter Hermes Furian

INTRODUCTION

The British couple, arms around each other, smiled broadly as they stood near the square side door of Chiesa di San Michele, the Church of St Michael in the mountaintop village of Savoca, Sicily. It's a five-minute stroll uphill from the iconic Bar Vitelli, a location familiar to every Godfather fan and the first stop for anyone who has decided to make the pilgrimage. No doubt the couple visited it first. Their tour guide snapped the photo and told them they were standing in the very spot where Michael Corleone and his Sicilian bride Apollonia knelt to accept their wedding blessing. Afterwards, the trio turned and walked back down the hill.

The village of Savoca is home to two locations used in the film. The Church of St Michael isn't one of them. A further walk uphill would have led them to the correct spot at Church of San Nicolò; they were unknowingly at the wrong location. Had the couple ventured independently, they could have sought guidance from a local, even though the villagers often colloquially term it the 'Church of Santa Lucia'. Recently, a new sign has been constructed to help clear up the matter.

Half a dozen years later, the memory of wanting to interject remains, but the potential impoliteness stopped me from doing so. The thought of that moment and the couple has crossed my mind over the years.

The confusion highlights the challenge of finding accurate information about Godfather filming locations in Sicily. Having watched the movies countless times and being obsessed with every detail, I embarked on my own extensive journey around the island. In preparation, I sought a comprehensive guidebook to meticulously plan my route. To my surprise, none existed. Despite the initial appearance of credible online information, deeper investigation revealed fragmented and inaccurate details on most websites. The dedication to precision often yielded to the pursuit of views and ad revenue. This discrepancy even contributes to the common misconception that scenes were filmed in the town of Corleone, leading disappointed visitors to arrive there every year under this mistaken belief.

Inspired by my personal journey and the lack of reliable resources, *The Godfather Lover's Guide to Sicily* is my endeavour to compile all the necessary information for enthusiasts to re-experience The Godfather films, whether in real life or from the comfort of their homes. This comprehensive guide includes side trips, film facts, scene analysis, and insights into Sicilian culture. The ultimate goal is to make your journey effortless. Drawing on my background as a Mediterranean archaeologist, I aim to provide a deeper historical context for the sites so that visiting these locations isn't just about retracing the film's narrative. The sites have retained much of their original charm, offering an immersive experience that feels like stepping into the films themselves.

The Godfather films were released in 1972, 1974 and 1990. NBC broadcasted a four-part miniseries, *The Godfather Saga*, in 1977. *The Godfather* and *The Godfather: Part II* were edited in chronological order with nearly an hour of deleted scenes. It became the most-viewed television movie when it aired, with over 100 million viewers. In 1992, *The Godfather Trilogy: 1901–1980* was made available; all three films were edited into chronological order with far more deleted scenes included. Various other versions exist. This book focuses on all three films as well as known deleted scenes.

This guide was written by leveraging a diverse range of source materials. Books (contemporary and historical), periodicals, academic publications, script drafts, deleted scenes and Francis Ford Coppola's own comments all contributed. Ira Zuckerman's publication, *The Godfather Journal*, proved invaluable in understanding the tension and emotional aspects of the production through a first-hand account. The 1970s archives of periodicals (Sicilian and otherwise) turned out to be a treasure trove of filming details and observations. Elbow's deep analysis of Sicilian government websites, often with unindexed pages, provided information I've not seen written elsewhere. I'm grateful to the bureaucrats who were so diligent in their notes and dedicated to archiving.

I hope the couple stumble upon this book and find inspiration for a return journey to Sicily.

Karen M. Spence
Mérida, México

THE GODFATHER: A DIFFICULT BIRTH

'And the Sicilian sequences really make the film, I think.'
Mario Puzo, author of *The Godfather*, in his autobiography *The Godfather Papers and Other Confessions*.

In the summer of 2022, the ancient Greek theatre of Taormina, Sicily, sets the scene for an emotional tribute to a masterpiece of cinema. The Mayor of Savoca, home to the iconic Bar Vitelli and the setting for Michael Corleone's first wedding, is ready to present a key to the city at the annual Taormina Film Festival. Local extras that took part in the production are seated in the audience. The recipient is the filmmaker Francis Ford Coppola, who made the Mayor's village instantly recognisable to cinema fans worldwide in 1972.

More than fifty years prior, the author Mario Gianluigi Puzo found himself in a less glamorous setting: a library in New York City. Gambling, plus the vicious cycle of debt, created pressure to write a book less for literary reasons and more out of desire to pay his bills. Inspired by real-life mafiosos, yet claiming to have never met one, the resulting novel sparked a film that has become a cultural phenomenon: *The Godfather*.

The Godfather films narrate the saga of the Corleones, an Italian-American mafia clan rooted in New York yet deeply tied to their cultural origins in Sicily. Unfolding over nearly eight decades, the trilogy serves as an expansive portrayal of how power, greed, and perceived injustice can corrode the American Dream. Some see the films as a nuanced exploration of the nexus between organised crime, politics, and unwavering family loyalty, while others interpret it as a narrative where a son relinquishes his humanity to embrace the family's criminal legacy. Perhaps for some men, *The Godfather* reflects a depiction of potent masculinity, a response to a world where they feel castrated by modernity or feminism – a sentiment heightened by the backdrop of the women's rights movement a decade before the first film's release. This is a possibility, mafia and Sicily. So effective at lending a veneer of glamour to the mafia that members themselves, at first opposed, adopted it as part of their culture. Before the film, the notion of the mafia as 'Men of Honour' didn't really exist. Coppola stated in a 1975 interview that the film wasn't about the mafia at all. Rather it is a Shakespearean tragedy similar to King Lear, a king and his three sons, centred around power and succession. He condemns the mafia lifestyle. The reality is that everyone has their own interpretation and personal lens. Sometimes travellers to Sicily, burdened by these stereotypes, struggle to perceive the island for what it truly is. Hopefully, this will change.

But birthing a masterpiece wasn't without its challenges.

Author Mario Puzo and Director Francis Ford Coppola. Paramount Studios

though one rarely voiced out loud. Maybe for some female fans, the fantasy of the take-charge male is at play. What remains indisputable is the audience's lack of repulsion at Michael Corleone's cold authority within a business that involves orchestrated violence. Power, it seems, possesses the capability to eliminate moral ambiguity beyond a certain threshold, earning him the audience's respect.

Nevertheless, the films have left an indelible mark on the collective cultural imagination when it comes to both the

Mafia interference during the making of The Godfather film

Francis Ford Coppola and his crew set up pre-production for *The Godfather* in Little Italy, New York City, on a cold morning in March of 1971. After a lengthy back and forth with studio bosses, the director got his wish to include the city as a backdrop to his scenes. Less expensive locations like St Louis were considered. The high artistic ambitions of the director didn't match the low budget dictated by the studio. Nevertheless, Coppola got what he wanted: about 90 per cent of the first movie was filmed in

New York and the surrounding area. The producers reigned in Coppola's creativity where they could. He never received the $5,000 needed to reconstruct the iconic Camel smoke-ring sign located on Broadway that would only be shown in the picture for a few seconds. Likewise, Robert Evans, head of worldwide production for Paramount Pictures and financier of the film, said in an interview that he would be overseeing the filming from day one. He felt studios were too relaxed in their approach to controlling productions. Coppola was offended by this remark. It was only the beginning of an adversarial relationship between the two men, and a future collaboration ended up in a courtroom.

Nevertheless, filming was to begin on 29 March but since snow flurries were predicted for 23 March, the producer Albert S. Ruddy moved the schedule up. The real snow never transpired. The scene between Michael and Kay, purchasing Christmas presents in front of the department store Best & Co., on Fifth Avenue, was filmed anyway, with the aid of a snow machine.

But the weather reports were the least of their worries at that point.

In the month prior, production is notified that the original location chosen for the Corleone compound, in

The first day of filming, 23 March 1971, in front of Best & Co. Paramount Studios

Manhasset, Long Island, has suddenly been tied up in a bureaucratic mess. The local government has mandated that a set wall that was to be built around the property must be taken down every night and reassembled in the morning. The labour cost for this would impact the budget, not to mention cause the loss of daylight shooting time. Rumours abound that the mafia has taken notice of the film. And they aren't happy. Eventually, Long Island will be abandoned for Staten Island, the location replaced with a Tudor-style home on Longfellow Road. The change of plans costs $100,000.

Joseph Colombo Sr., the powerful head of an organised crime family during the 1960s and into the 1970s, is concerned about image. Specifically, the tough guy, gangster stereotypes surrounding Italian-Americans. He has founded an organisation called the Italian American Civil Rights League to combat the portrayal. His son Anthony later took up the mantle. In the past, they have held rallies and even picketed the Federal Bureau of Investigations. As a result, US Attorney General John H. Mitchell has ordered Justice Department officials to stop using the terms 'mafia' and 'Cosa Nostra'. Now the League has its sights set on *The Godfather*. The League had made it clear: locations that collaborated in the film would be doing so at their displeasure. This had become frustratingly obvious to location coordinators. It also was made obvious to Al Ruddy, producer of the film, whose car windows had been shot out with a note left on the dashboard 'Shut down the movie – or else.'

Al Ruddy had a diplomatic solution. On 20 March 1971, *The New York Times* reported that during a sit down with the League, they reviewed the script together. All references to 'mafia' and 'Cosa Nostra' would be purged. Also, the proceeds from the première would be donated to the League. Paramount Pictures executives were incensed, claiming the meeting was unauthorised, but said they would remove the words based on the precedent set by the Attorney General. They were less willing to part with the première funds. Rumours spread that Ruddy may be fired. The producer stressed that the League started going door to door, urging local residents to now be friendly to the crew. Director Coppola knew to stay out of it and let Al do his job. He would later say, 'I always thought of these figures of the crime family sort of like the old myth of vampires, which a vampire can only come into your life if you invite him to step over your threshold.' Coppola never issued an invite.

The first day of shooting began three days later without any more interference. The League and its associated members became allies of the film. Soon after its release, they would adopt it as part of their own culture.

Coppola directs Al Pacino and Diane Keaton. Paramount Studios

Coppola films in Little Italy. Paramount Studios

The Director and the Don. Paramount Studios

The Godfather Films in Sicily

Mario Puzo was correct, the Sicilian scenes are some of the most memorable across all three films. They nearly didn't happen. With so much great footage already completed in New York plus the studio's ever-present concern with the budget, Paramount executives were reluctant to indulge Coppola's creative desire. They preferred to use the less expensive mountains of upstate New York instead. It was noted that Al Ruddy, during a lunch break in the studio's cafeteria, mentioned he was trying to get the airline TWA to fly the cast and crew to Sicily *gratis* in exchange for publicity. It didn't help that there were concerns about how the recent elections in Italy would impact the production. In the end, Coppola pushed back and prevailed, though he was only allowed to bring a skeleton crew. The sequences were the last to be filmed before it was all sent to editing. Al Ruddy would later comment that the Sicily filming was the most 'blissful' of the entire film for Coppola. He would later say of their time in Sicily, 'The shooting itself was fairly uneventful. Everything went like clockwork. We did our stuff and got out.'

Directing in Sicily. Paramount Studios

Filming in Sicily. Paramount Studios

SAVOCA

'Supra na rocca Sauca sta, sette facci'
Leonardo Sciascia, 1961.

The author Leonardo Sciascia was right to describe Savoca as the town of seven faces. From every direction, a new panorama and a fresh perspective can be seen. Even before the film *The Godfather* made it famous, this hilltop medieval village was regarded as beautiful.

Founded in the twelfth century, many believe the village is named after the elderberry plant (Norman '*savucu*'). An elderberry twig is even depicted on the town's medieval coat of arms. In 2008 it was officially recognised by the Association 'I Borghi più Belli

Savoca, Sicily. Dennis Jarvis, Flikr

d'Italia' as a 'borgo'. While in English this translates to 'village', the deeper meaning is that it has been recognised as an exceptional and ancient village that continues to maintain high standards.

Surrounded by vineyards, citrus trees, and pine woods, fortified with Norman era town walls and secured with an ancient gate, and home to several monumental buildings, it is no wonder the director Francis Ford Coppola felt Savoca would lend itself well to the authenticity of Michael Corleone's 1940s exile.

Bar Vitelli, Piazza Fossia, 7, Savoca, Messina

- **Scene(s) GF I:** *Michael Corleone, along with his bodyguards, enquires about a woman in the village he has seen. The bar owner is her father, Signor Vitelli, accompanied by his two sons. After some small talk, Michael informs him that he plans to wed his daughter Apollonia and asks to court her in the Old World fashion.*
- *Signor Vitelli and his family enjoy a lunch with Michael where he meets Apollonia, gifting her a necklace.*
- *Michael and Apollonia celebrate their wedding after exchanging vows.*

- **Scenes(s) GF III:** *A flashback scene, Bar Vitelli can be seen in the background of the wedding dance at the marriage of Michael and Apollonia.*

Background

Set on the Piazza Fossia, in the mountaintop village of Savoca, fans of the films are sure to recognise Bar Vitelli as the place where Michael Corleone proposed that he would marry. Not to the woman herself, but

to her family, in the traditional style of marriage proposal.

This is one of the few humorous scenes in the film, as Michael is unsure at first what arouses the anger of Signor Vitelli, the jealous father of the woman whose beauty hit him like a thunderbolt. He confides that he is an American, hiding in Sicily, and that a bounty exists for that information. This scene has its threatening side too, he warns Signor that Apollonia could either lose her father or gain a husband. This is Michael, son of the Godfather, now making his own offer that can't be refused.

Above: *Michael Corleone and Calo at Bar Vitelli.* Paramount Studios

Left: *The iconic Bar Vitelli.* Ramón Cutanda López, Flikr

Below: *Bar Vitelli.* Paramount Studios

> **Film Facts:** The director Francis Ford Coppola asked Saro Urzì, the actor who played Signor Vitelli, to straighten his suspenders with his thumbs when Michael speaks of marriage in order to let the viewer know that a transaction is taking place.

The Palazzo Trimarchi building sits on the remains of a noble palace built in the 1400s. The building is Neoclassical in design and constructed of lavic stone. It was renovated in 1773, as evidenced by the engraved keystone located above the front door. Regionally, it has been officially declared a Monumental Asset. Today, instead of the black awnings in the film, you will find a leafy trellis. The outdoor tables remain and the 'Itala Pilsen' sign can still be seen, popular with photographers.

   Fans may be surprised to discover that the bar was only opened commercially in 1963 and was left unnamed. The tiny, isolated village colloquially knew where to enjoy a Sicilian lemon granita served with zuccarata, a local biscuit topped with sesame seeds... or perhaps something stronger. It was Francis Ford Coppola himself who christened it 'Bar Vitelli' for the movie, a name that has become world famous over the last fifty years. Mrs Maria, the owner of Bar Vitelli, herself recalled making dozens of granitas per day for both the director, his family and the cast and crew between takes. It was a scorching hot mid-July and even fifty years later Coppola remembered the heat of Savoca in a recent interview.

> **Film Facts:** Key personnel arrived in Sicily on 22 July with the cast arriving on 24 July. The shoot was originally intended to be ten days long but had to be extended due to inclement weather. All scenes filmed in Sicily are under sunny conditions; this is meant to contrast with the darkness of the previous scenes filmed in New York City.

Today the bar remains much the same and contains a mini-museum of Godfather memorabilia and photos from the 1971 filming. The building offers 5 suites and functions as a boutique hotel should you wish to stay overnight at this iconic location. It is free to enter but customary to make a purchase, if only a shot of espresso at the bar.

   Directly in front of Bar Vitelli is the Piazza Fossia, which often appears smaller than it looks in the movies! Romance abounds in this tiny piazza; it is both where Michael presents Apollonia with a gift of a necklace and later where they hold their wedding reception.

Coppola directs Al Pacino for the courtship scene. Paramount Studios

Reception at Bar Vitelli, 'Itala Pilsen' sign in the background. Paramount Studios

Reception at Bar Vitelli. Paramount Studios

Inside Information: The local who was cast to play Signora Vitelli, Vincenza Cicala, was raised in the village and still lives there to this day. She often accepts interview requests; interestingly most of these come from either the United States or China. Some couples recreate their weddings in Savoca in the same manner as *The Godfather*, and will send her an invite. She's a local celebrity.

Signora Cicala is very friendly if you happen to meet her. When I asked her how she was selected for her role as Apollonia's mother, she cheekily replied that it was because she was the most beautiful woman in the village.

Another person who was an extra in the film, Vincenzo Pasquale, still resides in Savoca as well.

In the Piazza you cannot miss the steel silhouette of Godfather director Francis Ford Coppola, overlooking the hills and beyond to the Ionian Sea. It was created by the local artist Nino Ucchino and pays tribute to the

Coppola tribute by Nino Ucchino. Jonas Forth, Flikr

L' Asino Parlante *by Nino Ucchino.* Author's collection

filmmaker who brought worldwide notoriety to Savoca.

Curiously, right behind it is a large statue of a talking donkey, 'L' Asino Parlante', created by the same artist. For some change, you can hear it make grunting noises. While this may remind you of the donkey impression scene voiced by the character Spara in *The Godfather Part III*, there is no connection. The artist claims it is inspired by the animal itself, who toiled alongside the ancient peasant to produce food and serves as a nod to agrarian Sicily.

Did You Know?

At her wedding party, Apollonia can be seen serving white sugared almonds to each of her guests. These are known as 'confetti' in Sicily and are a wedding tradition across Italy and other countries as well. They are given to guests in multiples of either three or five as even numbers are considered to be unlucky. Three almonds are said to represent the bride, groom and future children while five almonds represent happiness, health, fertility, longevity and wealth. Some say the tradition, dating back to at least the Middle Ages, is symbolic of the bittersweet reality of life. Guests that eat the almonds are practising what is called 'auguri', in effect giving good wishes to the newlywed couple.

Church of San Nicolò (Chiesa di San Nicolò), Via S. Nicolò, 4, Savoca; locally called the Church of Santa Lucia

Scene(s) GF I:
- Exterior scenes of the wedding of Michael Corleone and Apollonia Vitelli.
- Procession of the wedding party to the reception at Piazza Fossia/Bar Vitelli.

Background

It is on the doorstep of the Church of San Nicolò we find Michael and Apollonia kneeling to receive their final marital blessing. They are surrounded by Michael's gun-toting, bullet-laden bodyguards and Apollonia's reserved-looking parents, a juxtaposition of business and family. Only the exterior of the building was filmed. The wedding procession continues down the cliffside street to Bar Vitelli for the reception, while rice is being thrown. The village band is playing a rendition of Antico Canto Siciliano, arranged and adapted by the director's own father, Carmine Coppola.

Marital blessing on the doorstep of the Church of San Nicolò. Paramount Studios

Wedding procession. Paramount Studios

Sicily Trivia: A lupara is a sawed-off, double-barrelled shotgun traditionally associated with Cosa Nostra. Its shortened barrel makes for easier concealment. The Italian word lupara means 'for the wolf' as this weapon was originally used for wolf hunting.

Located on one of the highest points of the village, the church was originally built in the thirteenth century. After an earthquake, it was renovated, and the current building presents itself with eighteenth-century architecture. For many, it appears like a Norman castle. For 600 years distinguished citizens of Savoca were buried in ossuaries underneath the

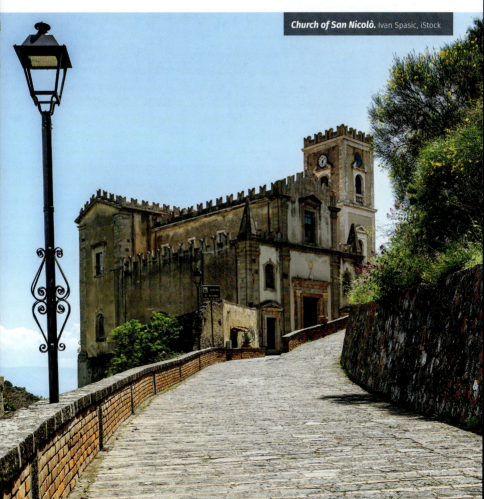

Church of San Nicolò. Ivan Spasic, iStock

Dioniso Di Morabita Andrea wine bar. Andrea Morabita

floor of the stone plaza in front of and in the side yard of the church, though the modern visitor will be unaware of this as it is unmarked. This was a common practice throughout Europe.

Following in the wedding party's footsteps you'll find several options to stop for a meal, coffee, or a glass of wine. Dioniso Di Morabito Andrea (Via San Michele 15), a wine bar owned by a former biologist, has a lovely view over the village and outstanding charcuterie boards. Anthony Bourdain held a crew meal here while filming his series *Parts Unknown* in June 2013.

'You can smell the garlic coming off the screen.'
Casting Director Fred Roos, 2007.

Did You Know?

Locals sometimes call this building the Church of Santa Lucia, or St Lucy's Church, which can be confusing for visitors! Don't be fooled, they are one and the same. The silver statue of Santa Lucia, the patron saint of the village, is housed within the church. It was created by an unknown Sicilian artist in 1666. The patronal Feast of

Feast of St. Lucia, Savoca. Andrea Morabita

St Lucia folk festival is held annually during the second Sunday of August and includes a live and dramatic retelling of the saint's martyrdom. The solemn commemoration is held each 13 December.

The Godfather Wedding Walk, Via S. Michele

Scene(s) GF I:
- Michael and his new bride Apollonia, led by the village band and trailed by wedding guests, leave the Church San Nicolò and walk to their reception at Piazza Fossia/Bar Vitelli.

Background

This very popular walk will allow you to follow in the footsteps of Michael and Apollonia after their marriage ceremony. Via S. Michele is a cliffside street with spectacular, romantic views over the hills and beyond, to the Ionian Sea.

Other Points of Interest

Museum of the City of Savoca, Via S. Michele, 1
Open daily from 10AM until 5PM, it will delight Godfather fans with an entire room dedicated to the making of the film. Artefacts include the original director's clapperboard donated to the museum

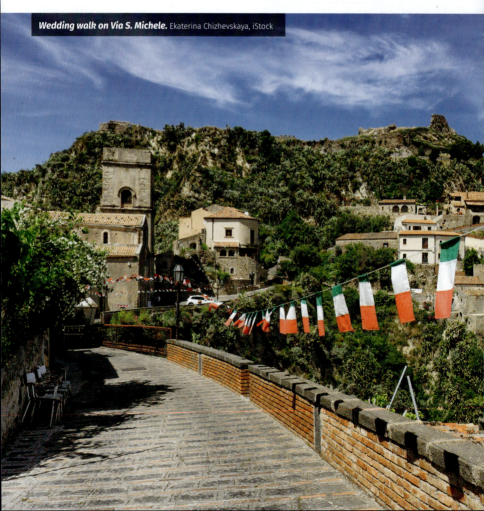
Wedding walk on Via S. Michele. Ekaterina Chizhevskaya, iStock

and a signed copy of the key to the city presented to Coppola in 2022. You'll also be able to see objects of daily life as well as ancient crafting tools, all providing a glimpse into Sicilian agrarian culture.

Capuchin Catacombs and, Via Cappuccini
Most famous for its catacomb containing seventeen preserved mummies from the 1700s, including the remarkably dehydrated remains of Abbot Antonio Garufi, who passed in 1795. He is dressed in his original clerical garments. The mummification process was carried out in the crypt of the Church of Santa Maria in Cielo Assunta but the mummies transferred here afterwards. Free to enter but donations are expected. Ring the bell to enter.

Church of Santa Maria in Cielo Assunta (The Mother Church of Savoca), Via Chiesa Madre
Don't miss this hidden gem! Dating to 1130, this monumental church is notable for its sixteenth-century fresco depicting the Assumption of the Holy Virgin into heaven. Note the fifteenth-century coat of arms above the main entrance door. This represents the Trimarchi family, the owners of the palazzo where modern day Bar Vitelli is built. The crypt below contains the putridarium; this is a temporary holding area for mummification. Several unusual wall niches can be found. These are desiccation seats; the central hole serves to collect the body fluids during the rudimentary mummification process which took about sixty days. The last mummification took place in 1876. The mummies can be seen at the Capuchin Catacombs on Via Cappuccini today. Additionally, the bell tower houses an ancient clock where, curiously, the numbers are arranged

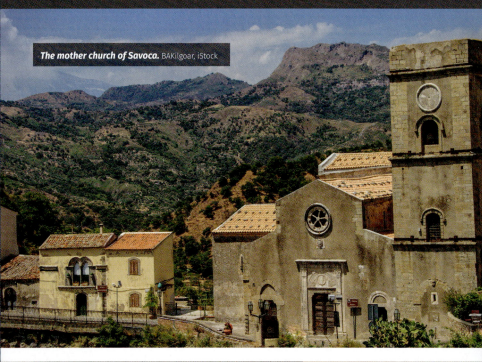
The mother church of Savoca. BAKilgoar, iStock

Example of a putridarium from nearby Forza d'Agrò. Mario Triolo

counter clockwise. This has been declared an Italian National Monument since 1910. Free, donations accepted.

Did You Know?

The clock of Santa Maria is extremely rare! Thought to be installed around 1641, not only were the numbers arranged counter clockwise but the sole hand (which only told the hours) also rotated in that direction. Called 'Italic time', the purpose was to indicate how many hours of daylight was left. This makes sense for two reasons: it was an agrarian society and the gates at either end of the village were bolted at sunset each night for defence reasons. This is the only similar clock found in Sicily and Southern Italy. There are only four other examples, all are located in Northern Italy. The system was complex and needed constant adjustment. It was replaced by the standard that we know today, which is called 'French time'.

Castle of Pentefur, Via Pentifurri

It's not easy to miss the dominating remains of Pentefur Castle, located on

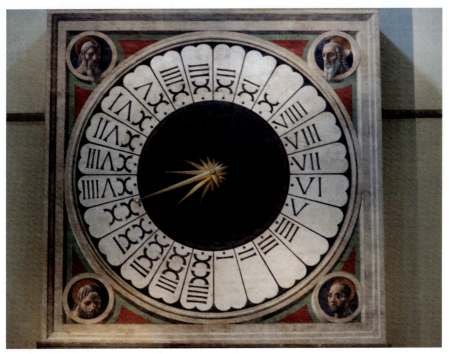

Italic clock, Florence. Allan Parsons, Flikr

one of the two hills upon which Savoca is built. Built originally as a defence fortress on a pre-existing Roman or Byzantine site, it was renovated around 1070 CE to become a residence for the Archimandrite of Messina. He was the head of an order of Greek monks who resided in Sicily. By the eighteenth century, it had fallen into great disrepair, hastened by a series of three earthquakes.

The name is a bit of a mystery. Medieval legend has it that it was built by five thieves who escaped from the prison at Taormina and used it as a hideout while raiding neighbouring villages. The less exciting reality is that Savoca was at one time divided into five districts and the castle name is more indicative of its location. Since 1885 it has been under the ownership of the Nicòtina family and is rarely open to the public.

Church of San Michele (Chiesa di San Michele), Via S. Michele 20

This church, built before 1250, is worth a visit. But don't fall victim to the misinformation that it was associated with the filming of *The Godfather*! It was never

Opposite: *Church of St. Michael.* Dennis Jarvis, Flikr

Below: *Castle of Pentefur.* Eugenio Nicola Scarcella, WikiCommons

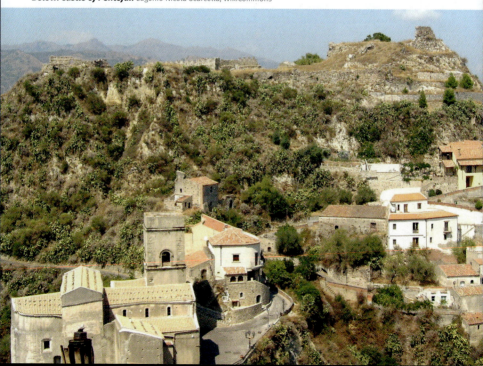

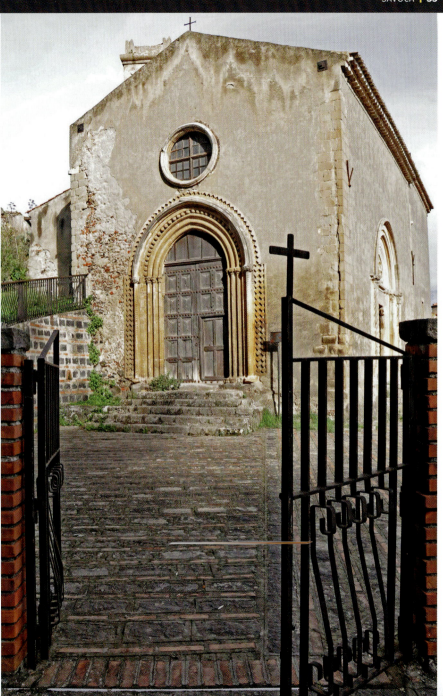

filmed or considered, contrary to what you may overhear guides telling tourists. In 2015, a major crowdfunding effort resulted in the restoration of the building and it now functions as a place of worship once again but it also hosts exhibitions from time to time. Most notable are the eighteenth-century wooden truss roof and the fresco depicting the Baptism of Jesus at the Jordan River.

Medieval Synagogue, Via S. Michele 20
Located a few steps from the Church of San Michele, it is unknown when the synagogue was built but documents tell us it existed in 1408. It was abandoned in 1492 due to the forced expulsion of Jews from Sicily and was never used for religious purposes thereafter. Free.

Savoca City Gate (Porta Della Citta di Savoca), Via S. Michele
Located on Via S. Michele, otherwise known as The Godfather Walk, you'll be sure to pass through this twelfth-century gate. During Norman times, a large city wall was built to defend ancient Savoca, with a gate at either end that would be opened at dawn and closed at sunset. Sadly, only this gate, with its sandstone arch, remains to be seen today.

Opposite: *Savoca city gate.* Dennis Jarvis, Flikr

Below: *Synagogue of Savoca.* Dennis Jarvis, Flikr

Calvary Hill, Panoramic Viewpoint, Via S. Giovanni 19

Want the best panoramic view of not only historic Savoca but Mt Etna, the Ionian Sea, the castle of Sant'Alessio Siculo and the nearby town of Saint Teresa of Riva? 'Calvario' is a twelve-minute walk (or three-minute drive) from Piazza Fossia/Bar Vitelli. The church itself is rarely open for visits with the exception of Holy Week activities. The route of the Via Crucis (Stations of the Cross) has been artfully dug into the rock and begins at Calvario. Regardless of whether the building is open or not, the view is worth the side trip alone. Dedicated Godfather fans are known to propose to their significant others at the iconic Bar Vitelli but if you are looking for a more private location in Savoca to pop the question, this would be a noteworthy suggestion.

Bifora Quattrocentesca (15th CE Medieval Mullioned Window), Via Chiesa Madre

Fans of architecture shouldn't miss the signposted Medieval window, constructed in the 1400s and located just past the mother church, Church of Santa Maria in Cielo Assunta.

The house itself is a private residence and not open to the public.

Side Trip

Less than forty-five minutes by car from Savoca is the seriously underrated Regional Museum of Messina, Viale della Libertà, 465, affectionately called 'Mume' by the locals. This art museum is the largest in all of Southern Italy. It chronologically displays art from the twelfth to eighteenth centuries, all of which were fortunate enough to survive the catastrophic earthquake of 1908, which saw many pieces of art lost. The early Italian Renaissance artist Antonello de Messina's work *San Gregorio Polyptych* from 1473 is on display.

However, the museum is most famous for owning two works by one of Italy's most famous painters, Caravaggio. These are *Adoration of the Shepherd* and *Raising of Lazarus*, an extremely dark work of art. For the latter piece, there is a legend that the painter asked local workmen to dig up a corpse in the beginning stages of decomposition to serve as a model. The local Catholic clergy, appalled at this, were keen to spiritually cleanse Caravaggio. When he appeared at church, they offered him a bowl of water. He inquired as to what they were offering. They replied that it was holy water and that it would wash away his venial sins. His response? It was of no use to him as all his sins were mortal ones.

It is not uncommon to confuse the intense works of painter Mario Minniti (Mume has four) with those of Caravaggio. Minniti was Caravaggio's friend and probably lover who often served as a model for the painter and was heavily influenced by his chiaroscuro techniques.

The Raising of Lazarus, *Caravaggio 1609.* Manuela Ideacrea, Flikr

FORZA D'AGRÒ

*'The climate's delicate; the air most sweet.
Fertile the isle, the temple much surpassing
The common praise it bears.'*
         Shakespeare, *Winter's Tale*
                Act 111, Scene 1.

Shakespeare isn't the only writer with a fondness for Sicily. The Italian poet and 1959 Nobel Prize winner for Literature, Salvatore Quasimodo, spent his childhood and early adult years in Forza d'Agrò, having moved there when his father was sent to help the local population after a devastating earthquake. This experience was said to have influenced his writings, where he wrote passionately about moral principles after observing death and suffering due to the fate of natural forces. Visitors sometimes describe Forza d'Agrò as unique, moody and historically intense when they first arrive after enduring the twisting and steep road to get there. The village itself is mostly inaccessible by cars, as its tiny lanes are too narrow. The quietness lends an eerie and ancient feel. It is easy to understand why both

Above: *Narrow lanes of Forza d'Agrò.* Miguel Virkkunen Carvalho, Flikr

Opposite above: *Forza d'Agrò.* Mario Triolo

Opposite below: *Forza d'Agrò.* Mario Triolo

Quasimodo and, nearly seventy years later, the director Francis Ford Coppola would feel so inspired to create literary and cinematic art respectively.

View of Mt Etna. Mario Triolo

Church of Santa Maria Annunziata e Assunta (the Duomo), Via SS Annunziata 8, Forza d'Agrò

Scene(s) GF I:
- In a deleted scene: very briefly Michael and his bodyguards walk past the square and church.
- Michael and his bodyguards walk through the church square. Michael asks, 'Where have all the men gone?' and is told they are all dead due to vendettas.

Scenes(s) GF II:
- Young Vito escapes his village hidden in a basket carried by a donkey while Don Ciccio's two henchmen, Mosca and Strollo, look on and wave, unaware.
- The donkey carrying young Vito walks down an alley to the left of the church, laundry hangs overhead.
- Vito and his wife Carmela exit the church after mass, with their three children.

Scenes(s) GF III:
- Michael and his now divorced wife Kay witness a wedding party exiting the church.

Forza d'Agrò. Mario Triolo

Forza d'Agrò has a long and storied history, first settled by the Greeks between 8 BCE – 5 BCE. The village name itself comes from the Italian word for 'fortress', and 'agrò' is a reference to the river that once nourished the entire agricultural valley. This 'fortress by the river' village started to form in the fourteenth century and is overshadowed by a Norman castle at its highest point. The village features atmospherically in all three Godfather films.

Background

The Church of Santa Maria Annunziata e Assunta, also known locally as the Duomo, is the most recognisable church from The Godfather trilogy. It makes an appearance in all three films. Few can forget the heart-breaking scene that took place in its square. The orphaned nine-year-old Vito Andolini, later to become Don Vito Corleone, is forced to escape the village of his birth hidden in a basket carried on the back of a donkey. His destination was America, where he would begin a new life.

The Duomo itself is no stranger to new beginnings. Dating from the year 1400, it was completely destroyed in an earthquake in 1648. Work began to rebuild it and the opportunity was taken to reorient the façade in a different direction. Less than fifty years later, in 1693, it was again devastated by an earthquake. The front of the church we see today, typical of Sicilian

Duomo (SS Annunziata). Mario Triolo

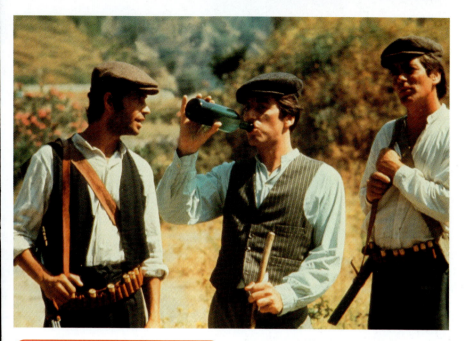

Above: *Michael and his bodyguards.*
Paramount Studios

Film Facts: The director Francis Ford Coppola had a difficult time casting Al Pacino, an unknown actor, for the lead role of Michael Corleone. The executives at Paramount Studios preferred to cast a more established actor, and Ryan O'Neal was favoured by the producer Robert Evans. Coppola has stated that he persistently envisioned Al Pacino's face in the scenes shot in Sicily, particularly the scenes where the character of Michael is walking with his two bodyguards. These shots that he references were later filmed mostly in Forzo d'Agrò.

Baroque architecture, is a result of the repair work dating from that time.

Usually open for tourists, the interior is noteworthy for a few reasons. Look for the painted crucifix; it was considered a miracle by the villagers (called 'Forzesi') when they saw it had survived the church collapse in 1648. The artist is unknown. In 2006, the Stations of the Cross were painted on the walls by Stefano Basile. He was inspired by a different piece of cinema. Basile specifically mentions the Mel Gibson film *The Passion of Jesus Christ* as his inspiration for their style.

Duomo (SS Annunziata). Mario Triolo

Film Facts: Mood is conveyed through the decorations of the church and the presence of a donkey. When young Vito is forced to leave the village of his birth hidden in the basket of a donkey, the church is unadorned. When Vito returns as a prosperous young man, the church is festooned with billowy curtains and beautifully decorated. A donkey with a confident young boy astride walks across the very same square from which Vito had hastily departed. In *The Godfather Part III* the church is decorated for a wedding; the village band is present. Kay takes this opportunity to tell Michael that their daughter Mary hopes to marry her cousin, Vincent. A donkey carrying a basket filled with oranges walks in front of them during this conversation.

Above: *The Duomo from above.* Ludwig14, Flikr

Right: *Pacino and Keaton, behind the scenes on* GF III. Paramount Studios

Beneath the church lies the crypt; remarkably, the Duomo and its churchyard have served as the village cemetery from feudal times until the nineteenth century.

While the village has four existing churches, the Church of Santa Maria Annunziata e Assunta is considered to be the Mother church of the village. Only the exterior of the church was filmed.

Inside Information: Want to visit the actual espresso and snack bar frequented by both the cast and crew while they were filming *The Godfather Part III*? Bar Eden on Piazza Cammareri is the place! The charismatic and proud owner is more than happy to talk to visitors about his 1990 experience. Several photos of Francis Ford Coppola, Al Pacino and other actors and crew eating at his establishment can be seen inside. Additionally, dozens of other photos taken during filming are viewable along with historic photos of the village itself. Don't miss this! Bar Eden's arancini is considered the best in Forzo d'Agrò and was a favourite of the director.

Did You Know?

The animated version of The Church of Santa Maria Annunziata e Assunta can be seen in the 2011 film *Cars 2* produced by Pixar Animation Studios for Walt Disney Pictures. Forza d'Agrò itself has been featured in over twenty-six films and television programs dating as far back as the 1948 Italian drama *Il Richiamo del Sangue* (The Call of the Blood).

Sicily Trivia: What is a vendetta? It's a term often associated with mafia and mob wars but generally a vendetta is a blood feud where the family of a murder victim vows to seek retaliation against the murderer or the murderer's family. The honour of the family is at stake if adequate vengeance isn't sought for a killed family member. The ancient Sicilian proverb 'Lu sangu lava lu sangu' ('Blood washes blood') sums up the philosophy. Vendettas are often prolonged, brutal and messy affairs since once a vengeful murder has taken place, a new vendetta is issued. Whole families can be killed due to retaliatory violence. In this case, Michael's question and his bodyguard's response demonstrate that the town itself has few living men left. It also tells us that the town or country is weak in enforcing its laws, otherwise murderers would fear being punished by authorities.

There is another bit of information that we can ascertain from this scene. Because there was such an imbalance between the number of women and the few living men remaining, it is understandable that Signor Vitelli was keen to make a marriage for his daughter Apollonia. Before Michael, the competition for eligible bachelors would have been intense, this being a time when most women would be expected to get married but so few men were available (and alive).

Michael learns about vendettas.
Paramount Studios

Church of Sant'Antonio Abate, Via Sant'Antonio 14, Forza d'Agrò

Scene(s) GF II:
- *Young Vito is packed into a basket fastened to a donkey in preparation for his escape, this takes place in the church square with the hills behind him. Abbandando and his wife tell Vito they are praying for him.*
- *Don Ciccio's henchmen, Mosca and Strollo, walk down a short flight of stairs, calling out 'Vito Andolini'. The church is directly behind them.*

Background

Only the most dedicated and eagle-eyed Godfather fans will notice that the Church of S. Antonio Abate is different from the church of SS Annunziata, because the scenes have been edited together to appear like the same location. Therefore, the Church of S. Antonio is never mentioned in connection with the films even though it features in two scenes in *The Godfather Part II*. If you decide to visit, you'll likely have the place to yourself! It is a ten-minute walk away from The Church of Santa Maria Annunziata e Assunta and is located in the Rocco district of the village. In the movie, the church was a ruin but it was restored in 1999 after an extensive reinforcement project.

> **Sicily Trivia:** Do not get this church confused with the church of the same name in nearby Taormina. Taormina offers its own Godfather location but none of their churches were ever filmed for the trilogy.

Today no religious services are carried out at the church though it occasionally offers exhibitions, usually works of art recovered from other religious buildings.

> **Sant'Antonio Abate, Patron Saint of Domestic Animals**
> Saint Anthony is the patron saint of rural life and farmers. He is also the protector of all domesticated animals. Curiously, it is thought that on his feast day of 17 January, all animals gain the faculty to speak. This comes from his connection to farming pigs and making an ointment from their fat to help heal shingles, known in Italy as 'fuoco di Sant'Antonio', or 'fire of St Anthony'. It is common in Italy to have your pets blessed on his feast day, especially in rural villages.

S. Antonio Abate. Mario Triolo

The scene was filmed on the left side.
Mario Triolo

Piazza de Triad, in front of the Chiesa Santissima Trinità, Via Vanellazza, 80, Forza d'Agrò

Scene(s) GF III:
- Michael and his now divorced wife Kay happen upon a violent puppet performance in the piazza.
- Michael and Kay dance in the piazza together, and live music is being played for a wedding reception.

Background

After ascending a sweeping staircase and passing beneath the unmissable fifteenth-century Gothic Catalan arch called Durazzesca Porta you'll find yourself in the piazza, or square, directly in front of Chiesa Santissima Trinità. It was built in 1576, on the site of a former, more ancient church. You'll be sure to notice its unusual pyramid-shaped spire directly above the bells.

Gothic Catalan arch Durazzesca Porta. Mario Triolo

Unusual spire of SS Trinità. Mario Triolo

Inside Information: Don't be confused if you hear the Chiesa Santissima Trinità (Church of St Trinity) referred to as the 'Church of St Augustine' or even 'the convent' by tour guides and even locals themselves! The Convent of the Augustinian Friars adjoins the church and both names are colloquially used for the same location.

Scene of the puppet show, Piazza SS. Trinità.
Mario Triolo

Only the piazza in front of the church was filmed and only for *The Godfather Part III*. It is in this square where Kay and Michael happen upon a puppet show that has a local audience. Just prior, we see the scene where Kay tells Michael that their daughter is in love with Vincent Mancini and Michael informs her that he would not allow their marriage as it is too 'dangerous'. In the following scene, Kay is seemingly enthused to see the puppets. However, the theme of the show is quickly revealed to mirror their real life; a woman has fallen in love with her cousin and her displeased father stabs her through the heart. Kay's face darkens and she remarks 'Honor, huh?' Clearly she is referring to their conversation about Mary and Vincent's relationship and seems unimpressed with the Sicilian tradition. This scene is not subtle.

After this, the pair dance in the piazza to a local wedding band and Kay reiterates that their son, Tony, will never join the family business.

Michael and Kay dance in the Piazza.
Paramount Studios

Sicily Trivia: Puppets and puppet shows are an important part of Sicilian heritage and cultural expression. This isn't the first time puppets are seen in The Godfather movies. In *The Godfather Part II*, we see a puppet on the wall of Anthony's bedroom, on the night of his First Communion party in Lake Tahoe. Also in *The Godfather Part II*, Don Fanucci observes a small puppet show taking place in the street at the Little Italy festival and declares it too violent. Most iconic may be the logo of the film itself, a hand holding a marionette cross, the strings attached to the word 'Godfather', alluding to who holds the strings of power.

In Sicily, marionette puppets are an ancient art form ('L'Opera deî Pupi', opera of the puppets) that visually enact tales, often romantic and/or violent in nature. Stories of war and bandits were often told. At times these performances allow for the re-enactment of true-to-life stories that otherwise are not meant to be spoken about without fear of repercussions. Some historians feel puppetry was a form of protest and transmission of information. This would have been helped by the fact that the puppet theatres were mobile; troubadours moved from village to village.

Sicilian puppets often depict violent scenes. Dennis Jarvis, Flikr

Visit of the Three Angels to Abraham by *Antonello de Saliba.* Mario Triolo

The interior of the church can be visited. Most noteworthy is the painting *Visit of the Three Angels to Abraham*, by Antonello de Saliba. This is located behind the high altar. Bread along with other food items are set upon a table and offered by Abraham to the angels. This custom of free distribution of bread is re-enacted at the biennial Feast of Saint Trinity.

> **Inside Information:** Unfortunately, the painting is a copy as the original was stolen in 1971 and never found.

Did You Know?

The increasingly popular Festa della Trinità (Feast of Saint Trinity) takes place on the first Sunday of June in odd-numbered years. This two-day event ends with the gifting of the village-made cuddura, a small doughnut, to all people in attendance. The villagers typically handmake them on Monday through Thursday the week before the Feast. Similarly, cuddura are also distributed on Easter Monday. The doughnuts themselves are round and braided

Don Vito's birthplace, exterior.
Author's collection

with a hole through the middle. They are stamped with the symbol of the church. The free distribution is said to reflect the tradition of offering hospitality to strangers, as seen in de Saliba's painting.

Casa de Il Padrino (the birthplace of Don Vito Corleone), Via Roma 5, Forza d'Agrò

Scene(s) GF I:
- In a deleted scene, Don Ciccio's henchmen, Mosca and Strollo, knock on the door and attempt to take Young Vito from his mother. She refuses and informs them she herself will bring her son to Don Ciccio's villa instead.
- In a deleted scene, Michael, accompanied by his bodyguards, knocks on the door of his father's birthplace. A woman passing by tells them that the family emigrated a long time ago and that no one remains.

Scene(s) GF III:
- Michael shows Kay the door of the house where his father was born.

Background

On Via Roma, a quintessential Italian village street with overhanging balconies and potted flowers, you'll find the house where Don Vito was born. Just the door was filmed, the interior of the home remains a private residence. Affixed to the wall beside it, look for a small picture of Al Pacino and Diane Keaton (Michael Corleone and his now divorced wife Kay) admiring the door, currently painted dark green. The

Film Facts: *The Godfather Notebook* is a book containing Francis Ford Coppola's thoughts on Mario Puzo's book *The Godfather*, upon which the film is based. In it, Coppola has added his notes to each page of Puzo's book. He himself said his notebook was more valuable when directing the film than even the script itself. On page 325 of Puzo's book, Coppola underlined the text stating that no relatives of Don Vito were left in Sicily and that they had all emigrated to America long ago. He notes, by hand, that this is '...[an] interesting point to make' and 'no relatives alive' in the margins. We later see this played out in the deleted scene.

Via Belvedere, near the corner of Via Roma, Forza d'Agrò

Scene(s) GF III:
- *Michael and Kay have parked their car on this street, Kay is surprised to receive flowers from a priest passing on a bicycle.*

owners are friendly but their home is not open for tours.

In *The Godfather Part III*, Michael tells Kay that this was the door that 'they' (meaning the local mafia chieftain) came to take his father as a boy to kill him. He seemingly expects sympathy but Kay seems unimpressed by this. Perhaps this is because Michael himself orders men to be killed in his role as a Godfather? Or maybe because Don Vito emigrated to New York only to become a Godfather and to murder people himself?

Background

Via Belvedere is a panoramic road that few visitors to the village will miss. The bicycle used in the scene was donated to the village and is on display along with a few photographs from the film production.

Above: *Forza d'Agrò, Via Belvedere.* Ludwig14, Flikr

Opposite: Godfather Part III *bicycle.* Author's collection

Inside Information: Fancy an incredible Sicilian lunch or dinner and want something off the beaten, touristy track with local pricing? It can be a little hard to find but the homey, family-run Ristorante 'O Dammuseddu at Via Dante Alighieri, 2, intersecting with Piazza Eros Cuzari 2, is worth the trouble. Look for their blue sign. The chef takes great pride in her food and is known for her mixed grill, mushroom risotto and wine cellar (mostly reds).

Prefer seafood at a restaurant with spectacular Ionian Sea views from its outdoor terrace? Trattoria Anni 60 on Via Santissima Annunziata 31 offers fresh fish and views of Calabria on a clear day.

Traditionally, a trattoria is considered to be a simpler and less expensive option than a ristorante but this distinction has become blurred over the last few decades. Occasionally, you will see an establishment called an osteria; the term has evolved from its humble roots to being considered the same as a ristorante. Simply look for the menu displayed outside the door to get a feel for what they serve and the price ranges.

FORZA D'AGRÒ | 59

Other Points of Interest

The Convent of Sant'Agostino, Piazza delle Triade, Via Vanellazza, 80, Forza D'Agrò
This austere building dates back to 1559, as evidenced by the engraving in the stone of the entrance arch. It adjoins the Chiesa Santissima Trinità. Augustinian friars (not nuns) were the occupants until the nineteenth century. As you enter, the room on your right (Santu Nicola) is sometimes used as a small museum. Very similar to the putridarium located in Savoca, a trapdoor leading from the room Santu Nicola into the basement reveals fifteen colourfully painted desiccation seats. Important friars, upon death, were 'seated' as part of the friar's funeral rituals. The dehydration process took about two months. A mass grave has also been found in the same location, where presumably less high-status friars were buried. The opening hours at this location are irregular.

Above: *Desiccation seats.* Mario Triolo

Opposite: *The former Convent of Sant'Agostino adjoins SS Trinità.* Mario Triolo

Il Castello Normanno (the Norman Castle), Via Annunziata SS, 121, Forza d'Agrò

Only the most surefooted tourists will want to make the trek up to the Norman Castle that dominates the village. The path up (follow the signs) is steep, narrow and not well maintained. The municipal authorities themselves refer to the climb up as mostly 'inaccessible', so consider yourself warned! If you do make the journey, you are not permitted to go inside the ruins though you can walk the hill until you reach the locked gate. You'll also enjoy the most spectacular views of the village. The Castle was built between the eleventh and twelfth centuries, making it one of the oldest in Sicily. Starting in the nineteenth century, it became the village cemetery, and several derelict gravestones can be seen. Previously, most burials took place at the Duomo.

Above: *The Norman Castle.* Mario Triolo

Opposite: *Stairs leading up to the castle.* Mario Triolo

Inside Information: Locals believe the castle is haunted by ghosts. On 24 July 1676, a real-life case of fratricide took place at the castle, reminiscent of the killing of Fredo by his brother Michael in *The Godfather*.

According to documentation, the French nobleman Don Antonio de Hox, occupant of the castle, had ambitions to become Lord of Forza d'Agrò. Reluctantly, he was told he needed to hand over the castle to his brother Giacomo, with whom he had a poor relationship. Under the guise of throwing a welcome feast, Don Antonio had his brother and his entire family chained and then murdered, the corpses never being found. Villagers claim the dragging sounds of heavy chains can be heard every 24 July since.

Did You Know?

Forza d'Agrò is famous for its live nativity scene and festival held between 26 December and the first Sunday of January. Preparations are begun several months in advance to 'recreate Bethlehem' as the locals call it. The actual nativity often has up to fifty village participants. Meanwhile, local products of wine, seasoned breads, olive oil and other treats are on offer. Artisans demonstrate ancient crafts and locals donate antique tools and utensils to ensure an authentic atmosphere. Only candles and firelight are allowed. Live nativity scenes are common across other parts of Sicily as well though this one is considered exceptional.

The Quartarello And Magghia, Ancient Neighbourhoods, Forza D'Agrò

The ancient part of the village is a mix of mostly abandoned houses and recently acquired houses that have been beautifully restored, often as holiday homes. The narrow lanes and overhanging balconies feel as though you have stepped back into the fourteenth century. This area may have the most Medieval 'feel' of all of the areas near Godfather filming locations, it feels like a movie set all on its own. It's only accessible by foot; be prepared to climb stairs. The houses, all made of local sandstone, are one or two storeys and generally only have two or fewer rooms. The tiled roofs are often collapsed. Locals consider this to be

Church of St. Sebastian, fresco depicting God. Mario Triolo

the heart of the village. If you walk just past the Duomo (The Church of Santa Maria Annunziata e Assunta) toward the Castle, you'll find yourself among its maze-like walkways. It can also be accessed from the Via Grutta.

Further north you'll find the Magghia, the oldest settlement in the village, settled in the 1100–1200s. It may seem unusual that the oldest side of town is located furthest from the sea. However, this was done on purpose to avoid visual detection from seafaring raiders. One of the most interesting places to visit is the ruin of Chiesa di San Sebastiano (Church of St Sebastian). Mostly collapsed, you can still see the deteriorated remains of a red and tan fresco in the domed apse of the building depicting God.

It is unknown exactly when the church was built but considering St Sebastian is the patron saint of the plague, it is possible it was built during one of the ten recorded epidemics that Forza d'Agrò experienced during the years of 1269–1523. Between the fifteenth and sixteenth centuries, four churches dedicated to St Sebastian were built within a twenty-five km distance of Forza d'Agrò in neighbouring villages; this gives some indication of the catastrophic impact of the disease.

MOTTA CAMASTRA

'Loved by artists for the monumental signs of overlapping civilizations... who in its fields, along its rivers, on its fortresses, in the ruins of its dead cities have reconstructed pages among the most suggestive of the history of peoples, this island of ours however, other beauties. Less flashy but no less worthy of being known...'
Enrico Calandra,
Sicilian Architectural Historian,
regarding Messina, 1927

Perhaps Enrico Calandra was thinking of Motta Camastra when he wrote this? We know for certain the cinematic artist and director Francis Ford Coppola felt so inspired by the 'less flashy' village that he decided to commit it to film.

Many people are surprised to learn that the real town of Corleone, Sicily, located about an hour south of Palermo, was never filmed. Instead, the stunning profile of Motta Camastra serves as a stand-in for Corleone in long shots of the village, while the other villages of Savoca and Forza d'Agrò were used for filming specific locations. All three villages are meant to portray the town of Corleone, the

Motta Camastra serves as "Corleone". Dan Tadd, Flikr

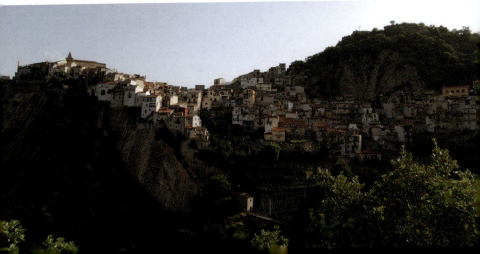

birthplace of Don Vito and now a refuge for his son Michael.

In some of the first scenes of Michael exiled to Sicily in *The Godfather*, we hear him tell Don Tommasino that he prefers to walk in the countryside instead of using the Don's car. The viewer is soon offered a panoramic shot of an ancient village high on a hill, church bells ringing in the background. Calo, his bodyguard, helpfully points out to Michael the name of their destination: 'Corleone'.

There are several reasons why the director and crew decided not to film in the real-life Corleone. During location scouting, Coppola found that Corleone had become too urbanised and built up to replicate the 1940s Sicily they wanted to portray in the first film. Additionally, 1970s Corleone was in the grip of organised crime. Coppola and his crew were asked to leave the town before sunset after being made aware that its use as a film location would be unwelcomed.

There is quite some confusion, especially online, regarding which village served as 'Corleone' in the scene where Michael sees it from afar for the first time. Usually, every village *except* Motta Camastra is named! The village today is known for its agrotourism and outdoor activities and doesn't especially promote its participation in the film. However, Godfather fans should know that Motta Camastra had its own brief part to play in *The Godfather*, in cultivating the image of Corleone in the movie and is 'no less worthy of being known'.

Motta Camastra, Views from the SP6 as you ascend, Messina

Scene(s) GF I:
- *Michael and his bodyguards, Fabrizio and Calo, are walking in the countryside; high on a hill they see the real-life Motta Camastra, Calo indicates that it is 'Corleone'.*

Background

Mario Puzo, the author of *The Godfather* book, specifically describes Michael's walks: '...the most striking thing in Michael's eyes was the magnificent beauty of the country... houses built like ancient Roman villas... On the horizon the bony hills shone like picked bleach bones piled high... and sometimes he walked as far as the town of Corleone, its eighteen thousand people strung out in dwellings that pitted the side of the nearest mountain... built out of black rock quarried from that mountain.'

Given the description, it is easy to see why the director Francis Ford Coppola was keen to film Motta Camastra, from the town's south side, to represent Puzo's vision of what Corleone would look like on its first impression.

Puzo's book describes the landscape as parched but also fertile, truly reflective of Motta Camastra's bucolic

Above: *Michael and his bodyguards, Fabrizio and Calo, lobby card.* Paramount Studios

Below: *Parched but fertile landscape.* Miguel Virkkunen Carvalho, Flikr

reality. Rather than focus on its connection to *The Godfather* as we see with the other two stand-ins for Corleone (Savoca and Forza d'Agrò), the village is promoting agrotourism these days.

> **Film Facts:** When Coppola and his crew left Corleone, they settled into Taormina to scout new film locations. While there, Coppola befriended the Sicilian Baron Gianni Pennisi, a well-known painter. It was Baron Pennisi who suggested the more suitable locations that we now recognise from the films as 'Corleone'. The Baron's own palatial estate was later filmed in *The Godfather Part III*.

Did You Know?

The people of this tiny village are known as Mottesi. The population is less than 600.

> **Bridge of Seven Arches, Graniti (hamlet), Motta Camastra, Messina**
>
> **Scene(s) GF I:**
> - In a deleted scene, Michael and his bodyguards see a Communist parade near the hamlet of San Cataldo.

Bridge of Seven Arches. Timeo, iStock

Background

In a deleted scene, Michael and his bodyguards observe a separatist parade; the participants are carrying red Communist flags. The crowd walk through a dry riverbed and under the arches of a large railway bridge. This scene was filmed at the Bridge of Seven Arches near the charming commune of Graniti.

In reality, the bridge was built by Fascists during World War II. The Germans endeavoured to blow it up as they were exiting Sicily in 1943, having been beaten back from the Allied invasion the month before. This effort was thwarted by a citizen of Motta Camastra who tampered with their explosives and saved it.

Visitors today can drive over the bridge. It is located in the countryside next to Strada Provinciale 7 (SP7), 11, 98036 Graniti, eight miles from Giardini Naxos (look for the blue sign).

Superfans may be interested to know that the opening scene of *The Godfather Part II*, Vito Andolini's funeral and Paolo's shooting death, was filmed nearby. Travelling along SP7 toward the tiny commune of Graniti (a four-minute drive) the mountain range and dry river bed are recognisable to the driver's right side.

> **Film Facts:** In the scene immediately following the view of Motta Camastra as Corleone, we hear Michael ask 'Where have all the men gone?' to his bodyguards as they walk. On the wall, there are plaques commemorating men who have died in vendettas. Eagle-eyed viewers will also notice a red Communist flag poster affixed. The flag reads 'PCI', which stands for the Italian Communist Party. In Francis Ford Coppola's notes about this scene, he specifically writes that he wanted 'a sense of the Communist party in posters, etc.' Michael's exile to Sicily occurred just a few years after World War II ended.

Above: *Post-war exile of Michael Corleone.*
Paramount Studios

Other Points of Interest

Alcantara Gorges, Via Nazionale SS 185

Hiking, river trekking and body rafting are all available in the ice-cold and clear waters of the Alcantara River. The basalt canyons on display are a consequence of the river flowing through hot volcanic lava flow from Mt. Etna, creating fractured-looking rocks reminiscent of a lunar landscape. While you can pay to take the lift, look for the municipal sign! This is the free entrance, but you will need to descend about 200 stairs.

Opposite: *Alcantara Gorges.* Jamie Tarallo, iStock

A few volcanic caves can also be seen if you are willing to make the hike. Grotta dei Cento Cavalli (The Cave of a Hundred Horses) is known for its spectacular size. It is most easily accessed by turning left on Contrada Finaita from SS185. From there you will need to hike for a few minutes to see it.

The Walnut Festival, Motta Camastra

This very popular event takes place during the first week of October each

year. Motta Camastra is one of the largest producers of walnuts in Sicily. Its production is helped by a few factors: its exceptionally fertile soil thanks to the frequent eruptions of Mt Etna, the favourable microclimate of the region and, lastly, its elevation of over 700 meters above sea level. Scientific studies have shown that Motta Camastra walnuts contain a hundred times more selenium (an antioxidant) than walnuts grown in other parts of Italy and even California.

The harvest is done manually in September and October. Tastings of their renowned giant walnuts, oil, local cheeses and sausages, and even walnut wine, are on offer.

Did You Know?

Sitting under a walnut tree for extended periods may cause a headache or rash. The tree produces a mild poison called juglone to protect itself from being eaten by insects and also to prevent other plants from growing beneath it, forcing the tree to compete for soil resources. If you complain of a migraine, locals may ask if you visited the tree fields.

Le Mamme del Borgo, Civic Centre, Via Simone Neri 4, Motta Camastra

In keeping with the village initiative toward agrotourism, a group of 'mothers of the village' have developed a culinary experience. They will cook a large lunch or dinner consisting of local dishes while village musicians play and sing Sicilian songs. All materials are sourced locally. The most recent menu included the labour-intensive macaroni 'alla Norma' and arancini with wild fennel! This experience must be booked in advance through their email lemammedelborgo.mc@gmail.com or through their Facebook page. The Motessi chefs are happy to answer questions about village life and are known to set the record straight that their village was the true inspiration for Corleone.

Opposite: *Walnuts from Mt Etna.* Rosario Scalia, iStock

Right: *Le Mamme del Borgo.* Le Mamme del Borgo

Sicily Trivia: No doubt you'll enjoy many memorable meals in Sicily. You may even hear the term 'cucina povera', which translates to 'kitchen of the poor' but in reality is a concept found the world over: it's about making great food from simple, high-quality ingredients. The Italians seem to have perfected the concept and your visit to Sicily will prove it; the Sicilians combine Italian staples with local island products such as sardines, tuna and chillies.

Sometimes visitors find the menu and course order to be a little confusing. One thing to remember, Sicilians don't expect you to order from every category unless you are very hungry. Most people, even Italians, will choose either a pasta dish or a meat dish. Here's a handy guide to help:

The first course served is usually the 'antipasti', which translates to 'before the meal' in Italian. These are your starters or appetisers. It involves cold dishes such as meats, cheeses, anchovies, stuffed artichoke hearts, aubergine (eggplant) that are often fried, baked or grilled and peppers in oil. 'Caponata' is a very popular starter, more like a sweet and sour salad, consisting of aubergine, onions, tomatoes, bell pepper, brined olives, vinegar and capers. It's hard not to overeat because there is so much selection and it is common to receive a mix of a little of everything.

The next course is called the 'primi'; think of it like the first main course. It often involves pasta such as linguine al limone, spaghetti al nero di sepia (with black squid sauce), and other kinds of pasta, some with meat and seafood and some without.

After this, we move on to the 'secondi', this is the protein course and in Sicily, fish is the primary protein on the menu. Local favourites include 'pasta con le sarde' (pasta with sardines) 'neonata a pastelle' (small fried fish), 'grigliata mista' (mixed seafood grill) as well as dishes such as 'salsiccia' (spicy sausage with fennel) or 'coniglio' (rabbit). Don't be surprised if this dish is not accompanied by a vegetable or anything else. If you would like a side dish, look for 'contorni' on the menu. Sometimes you need to specify you want it served with your secondi otherwise it may be served after! The most common contorni is usually a raw salad or steamed vegetables.

Lastly, save room for the 'dolce', often called the dessert course. Typical Sicilian desserts tend to be exceptional. 'Cassata' is an ancient Sicilian speciality; it's a sponge cake, ricotta and candied fruit. 'Sfogliatell'e are sweet ricotta turnovers. But you can always turn to your waiter and say 'I'll take the cannoli.'

A 'caffe' (post-dinner espresso) or 'digestivi' (after-dinner liqueur such as limoncello, grappa or amaro) is often ordered to complete the meal.

When you are ready to pay, you will need to ask for the bill ('il conto'). It's considered rude for the server to bring it to your table unsolicited. Don't be surprised to see a 'coperto', a cover charge, of about £1–3 per head on your bill. This covers the bread, oil, vinegar, salt and pepper brought to the table and is a widespread, non-negotiable charge throughout Italy. Some places, especially in mainland Italy, have banned the coperto because it is so unpopular with tourists but it is still the norm in Sicily. Don't feel that you are being taken advantage of! Lastly, look to see if a service charge ('servizio') has already been added. This is considered the gratuity. If not, 10 per cent is considered to be a good gratuity.

Buon Appetito!

Dinner in Italy. Nina/Flikr

TAORMINA AND SURROUNDS

'The Sicilian people embraced us... I loved their honesty, openness and hospitality.'
Al Pacino, reflecting on filming on location in Sicily.

Taormina is known for a great many things: its ancient Greek theatre, its annual film festival, its proximity to one of the most active volcanoes in the world, its spectacular views over the Ionian Sea and, yes, its hospitality. It's an ancient city founded over 2,400 years ago. In fact, glamourous Taormina is often referred to as the Riviera of Sicily.

The city has long attracted celebrities, artists and authors; travel books written about the city dating as far back as 1773 exist. The author Oscar Wilde stayed for a month in 1898, at the Hotel Victoria on Corso Umberto 81, which is still in business today. He was great friends with the resident Wilhelm von Gloeden, famous for his photography of the male form. In fact, cultural historians describe Taormina as historically attracting 'male refugees from more repressive climates' due to the open-mindedness of its residents. You'll find this honest and welcoming attitude still holds true today, as Al Pacino pointed out when speaking of his time filming in Sicily.

It is also where many Godfather fans may choose to base themselves on visiting various filming locations. The elegant Belmond Villa Sant'Andrea is where Francis Ford Coppola and the key cast and crew stayed when filming all three films. However, there is plenty of choice in this resort town! The shooting locations of Savoca, Forza d'Agrò, Motta Camastra, Castello Degli Schiavi and Mascali as well as the major filming locations described in *Chapter 6: Acireale and Surrounds* are all within a forty-minute driving distance of Taormina, making it a convenient basecamp.

Castello Degli Schiavi, SP 71i, 11, Fiumefreddo di Sicilia, Catania

Scene(s) GF I:
- Michael and his bodyguards pack gifts for Apollonia and her family into a car in the courtyard before driving out of the gates, Don Tommasino observes this.
- Michael and Apollonia enjoy their wedding night together in a bedroom after their marriage.
- Michael teaches Apollonia how to drive in the courtyard, Don Tommasino arrives with news of Sonny's murder.
- Michael stands on the balcony and instructs Fabrizio to prepare the car for him to drive.
- Michael looks for Apollonia in the kitchen, where he finds his bodyguard Calo eating breakfast.
- Michael walks down a staircase and witnesses Fabrizio leaving the property and subsequently Apollonia's death by car bombing.
- In a deleted scene, Michael, lying inside on a bed, becomes conscious and immediately asks about both Apollonia and Fabrizio.

Scene(s) GF II:
- Young Vito, with his wife and children, arrive at Don Tommasino's villa where they enjoy a meal in the courtyard.

Scenes(s) GF III:
- Michael meets with Don Tommasino in the courtyard, Vincent Mancini, Calo and others are in attendance. Michael introduces his now-divorced wife Kay to his former bodyguard Calo, in the courtyard.
- Michael and Kay have a scene inside, in the same bedroom of his wedding night with Apollonia decades prior.
- Michael and Kay have a meal in the dining room, Calo interrupts by opening a door from an adjoining room.
- Michael, an old man, dies in a chair in the courtyard.

Background

Castello Degli Schiavi, the stand-in for Don Tommasino's villa, is a property that has the distinction of participating in all three of the Godfather films, with scenes being filmed both inside and outside of the rural Sicilian Baroque castle. The house is so instrumental in telling the story that it could almost be considered a character in its own right. The castle is located in the commune of Fiumefreddo di Sicilia, which gets its name from the river that runs through it. 'Fiumefreddo' translates

Castello degli Schiavi, Castle of the Slaves. Andrej Antipin, Flikr

to 'cold river', a reference to the fact that the river is fed by the snow melts of the nearby volcano Mt Etna. It also has a lot of history and legend surrounding it which can be challenging to disentangle!

The 'Castle of the Slaves' was built between 1750 and 1756 with additions added in the eighteenth and nineteenth centuries. It sits on eleven hectares of citrus groves and is only a twenty-minute walk to the sea. Most noticeable is the loggia atop the building, a sort of rooftop terrace, whose purpose was for feudal managers to keep an eye on their workers in the fields. This loggia contains two life-sized Moors statues, both looking wide-eyed onto the farmland, reminding the workers that they were being watched.

> **Sicily Trivia:** Sicily accounts for 90 per cent of Italian lemon production.

What is the legend and what is the truth? Legend has it that a doctor in Palermo was granted the land to build the castle after saving the son of the Prince of Palagonia from the plague. The doctor built the fortified castle; he and his beautiful wife Rosalia lived there. One day, Turkish pirates ('Moors' but translated to Sicilian it means 'slaves') landed at the beach, ransacked the castle and took the couple as prisoners, intending to sell them into slavery. Fortunately for them, Rosalia's lover came to their rescue, freeing them from the pirates. As an offering of thanks to God, they constructed the loggia atop the castle we see today. Two stone statues depicting Moors/slaves are located there, their eyes are looking out toward the sea, hoping one day to be released from captivity.

The reality is a bit less sexy. A doctor received the lands and noble title as gratitude for his help fighting the plague in 1743. However, prior to the legend, the palace was referred to as 'casteddu di scavi' with 'scavi' meaning 'excavation', specifically of a large lava stone quarry that the family owned. Thus the toponym for excavation has been corrupted to mean 'slave'. As legends often do, the tale sounds better than the historical reality.

Did You Know?

Each corner of the castle has a turret. Be sure to look for the ears and eyes sculpted onto some of them. These can look quite out of place unless you know the history! Castello Degli Schiavi was a feudal estate. These symbols visually reminded the peasants that the eyes and ears of the masters were both watching and always listening. They were a visual reminder of baronial control.

Notice the eyes and ears motifs on the tower. Jonas Forth, Flikr

Sicily Trivia: Feudalism, sometimes referred to as the 'manorial system', was only officially abolished in Sicily in 1812, having existed in various forms for 800 years. However, extinguishing the practice itself took quite a while longer and was not without friction. With the transfer of baronial lands to private citizens, accounts and disputes needed to be adjudicated on and settled. Yet Sicily had very few police and little courtroom infrastructure, especially outside of the cities. As a consequence, many people started to turn to nonofficial persons and private armies to settle their disputes. Some scholars believe that the origins of the mafia started here; these private armies evolved into patron/client relationships. However, evidence exists as far back as ancient Roman times for the mafia as we understand it today. Research is ongoing.

Behind the scenes: Coppola and his family, Pacino, Corrado Gaipa, Gordon Willis and others.
Paramount Studios

Franco Platania, Baron of Santa Lucia, owns the property and still lives there today. He was living on the estate when all three Godfather films were shot. The castle itself has two floors. Historically, the first floor was used to store food produced in the fields while the family lived on the second floor, accessed by an external staircase. Today the Italian Baron still resides on the second floor but the first floor consists of eight rooms and houses memorabilia mostly related to the Godfather movies.

Inside Information: The Baron was paid three million Italian lire per day for thirty days of filming of *The Godfather*; this would be about 1,500 Euros in today's money. He met most of the cast and crew and remarked about Robert De Niro: 'De Niro was the nicest, always ready for a smile and a joke. It put you at ease. We became friends right away.'

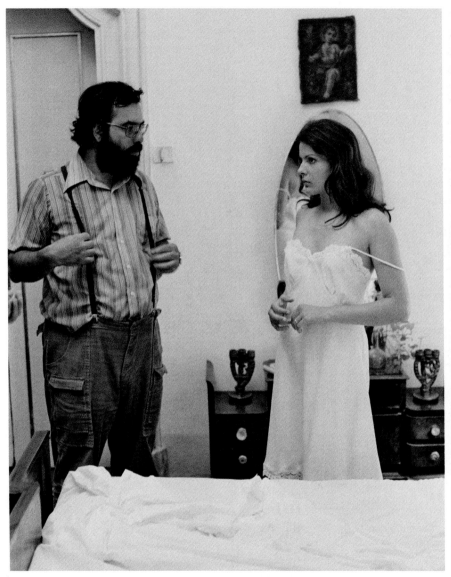

Above: *Coppola directs Simonetta Stefanelli for the wedding night scene.* Paramount Studios

Opposite: *Pacino and Stefanelli, wedding night at Castello degli Schiavi.* Paramount Studios

The three scenes set in the bedroom (Michael and Apollonia's wedding night, the deleted scene where Michael becomes conscious and, years later, Michael's dialogue with Kay in *Part III*) are confirmed by the director, Francis Ford Coppola, as having been filmed inside the castle and not at a separate location.

Speaking of the wedding night, many viewers are struck by the quietness

Apollonia learns to drive. Paramount Studios

of the scene. There is no dialogue between Michael and Apollonia as he turns from the window and kisses his new bride. This effect was intentional. The courtship of Apollonia and the wedding had music playing throughout. The only dialogue the viewer hears is Apollonia saying 'Grazie' ('thank you') when she receives the necklace from Michael. The director's notes say that he wanted the wedding night to be a 'coda' to the courtship and festivities, a muted conclusion to a widely celebrated wedding. The juxtaposition of the previous scenes filled with music and then the 'coda' of the quiet wedding night enhanced the sense of intimacy that needed to be portrayed and made the scene memorable.

> **Film Facts:** In the third draft of *The Godfather Part III* written by Coppola and Puzo, Michael and Kay end up making love in the same bedroom as Michael's wedding night with Apollonia. The film shows us quite a different story though, one where the couple never truly reconcile, and Kay seems angry and resentful throughout.

During their brief marriage, we see Michael attempting to teach his new wife how to drive. They never leave the circular driveway of Castello Degli Schiavi, instead, they drive around the water well, located in the middle of the courtyard and still in place today. There is a reason for this: Michael's wedding had drawn so much attention to his location in Sicily that the couple could not leave the fortress due to fears for their safety. Don Tommasino arrives to confirm this as well as to give Michael the news about his brother Sonny's murder.

Scene Analysis: Fans of the films will often debate if Apollonia would have been a better wife to Michael than Kay, his American-born, opinionated second wife. In contrast, Apollonia is often considered by the viewer to be a subservient village girl who would have been raised to be obedient regardless of her husband's occupation. While the later part is believable, the scene just before her death may indicate that she had as much a mind of her own as Kay did.

We get a glimpse of this when Michael is looking for Apollonia; the first place he thinks to check is the kitchen. The book tells us that Michael thought to himself 'She was most likely in the kitchen preparing his breakfast with her own hands...'

Yet she wasn't in the kitchen cooking. Instead, we find Apollonia in the driver's seat on the morning that she died, a choice she made on her initiative and clearly without asking permission from anyone.

We also see her push back when Michael teases her about her English skills. She replies in English with the (disordered) days of the week, and immediately says 'Come on! Let's go!' She further interrupts his conversation with Don Tommasino. Some viewers will interpret this as childish behaviour, yet her behaviour before her marriage was measured and mature.

Her tragic death by car bombing moments after often obscures the difference between the stereotype of a woman Michael believed he had married and perhaps the type she really was: wilful and confident in her agency. It's interesting to note that when Francis Ford Coppola was adapting and revising Mario Puzo's book for the movie, he crossed out several descriptions of Apollonia that advanced a subservient narrative. When Puzo wrote about Apollonia's virginity as being a 'premium', Coppola crossed it out with a pen and added a note in the margin: 'bullshit about virginity'.

It is up to the viewer to decide, but Apollonia and Kay may have much more in common than one would think. Both married Michael knowing his involvement in organised crime and both women also made choices without feeling the need to seek his approval.

Many fans of the movies will remember that Michael Corleone dies in a chair in the courtyard of the castle, alone, in *The Godfather Part III*. That chair has been left in the same spot and guests are invited to sit in it if they would like to have a photo. The external staircase that Michael descends just before Apollonia's tragic death is also available to see. The tour of the castle also includes the upstairs balcony where Michael fatefully asks his bodyguard to prepare his car.

The Godfather wasn't the first film to make use of Castello Degli Schiavi. In 1968, the famed Italian director Pier Paolo Pasolini shot some scenes of his film *L'Orgia* here. Most recently in 2022, the HBO series *The White Lotus* also made use of the property.

> '*I met him, I married him, I died.*'
> Simonetta Stefanelli, the actress who portrayed Apollonia, sums up her role in *The Godfather*, in a 1997 interview.

Film Facts: The first time the viewer sees the castle is when Michael and his bodyguards are loading the car with gifts to court both Apollonia and her family. Don Tomassino is also present, using a cane, and was previously seen in a wheelchair at the wedding. The part was played by three different actors since Don Tomassino was portrayed in all the films during different stages of life: young, middle-aged and elderly. In *The Godfather* the actor Corrado Gaipa assumed the role of the middle-aged Don. In real life, he also used a cane and was later wheelchair-bound. Unfortunately, the actor was unable to reprise his role as the elderly Don because he died the year before *The Godfather Part III* was filmed.

Inside Information: Don't show up at the gate and expect to be let in! If you ring the bell, there may be no response. Castello Degli Schiavi is a private residence and is not the easiest Godfather filming site to visit. Even the address given online for the estate is wrong. On SP 71i, 11, visitors will see a lava stone gate with an angry Saracen face sculpture and seashell above it. The property is viewable through this. There are no signs.

However, the Baron conducts all the tours himself if you are lucky enough to book one, which you will need to do through a third-party tour guide. You are usually expected to pay cash, currently 25 Euros per person in addition to whatever your chosen guide charges. The castle does offer weddings and events and seems keen to promote this over tourism. Currently, there is no restaurant or café in the courtyard as fictionally depicted in the HBO series *The White Lotus*, Season 2. Plan ahead to see this location!

Taormina-Giardini Naxos Railway Station (Stazione di Taormina-Giardini), Via Nazionale, 43, Villagonia, Messina

Scene(s) GF III:
- *Kay arrives at Bagheria railway station in Palermo and is greeted by Michael, Connie and her daughter Mary.*

Background

While the original railway station was inaugurated in 1866, the station we see today and in *The Godfather Part III* was built between 1926 and 1928. It's located about a kilometre from the village of Giardini but the name 'Taormina' was added since it's located within the municipality and serves both communities. It is recognised for its beautiful and photogenic Art Nouveau Liberty style, black and white tiled floor, wrought iron canopies and terraced location overlooking the Bay of Naxos.

It looks the same today as when it was filmed in the early spring of 1990. In this scene, we see Kay

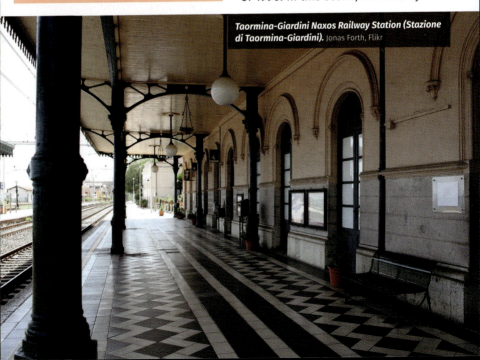

Taormina-Giardini Naxos Railway Station (Stazione di Taormina-Giardini). Jonas Forth, Flikr

arriving by train to Palermo and the station has been renamed 'Bagheria' according to the overhanging sign. Bagheria does exist in real life, it is located about twenty-five minutes from the Palermo opera house where Anthony Corleone will make his artistic debut as a singer. It's surprising to hear Kay mention, after exiting the train, that she had never been to Sicily before.

With its crenellated towers, the station appears like a castle. The inside of the station, especially the painted ceiling completed by Palermo artist Salvatore Gregorietti, is as spectacular as the outside and well worth a visit.

To make room for the station, the sixteenth-century Villagonia Castle as well as a chapel was demolished.

Regardless of its affiliation with the Godfather trilogy, this unique railway station is considered a tourist attraction in its own right.

Sicily Trivia: The Art Nouveau Liberty style was a popular architectural style in the early 1900s. At the heart of it, it seeks to make functional spaces (like railway stations) beautiful, uniting utility and art. There are several examples throughout Sicily, including civic buildings.

Inside Information: Find yourself in Taormina and fancy a pizza? You are in luck! Pizzeria Villa Zuccaro is not only set in a beautiful seventeenth-century villa but the chef is the master pizza maker, Corrado Bombaci, who won the World Pizza Championship – Pizza Without Borders competition in 2023 as well as the European Championship of 2019. It's open daily at Piazza Carmine, 5. They also own the nearby La Napoletana Pizzeria, Via D'Orville, 1/b (Piazza Varò), and cook using only Neapolitan dough. The crust is soft, foldable and features an elevated edge called a 'cornicione'.

Vegetarians, vegans and those with gluten-free diets will be very pleased to dine at the sumptuously located Rosmarino Ristorante, Via Bagnoli Croci, 88/B. Those dietary options are available across all courses, from starters to desserts. They also serve fish and meat dishes, prepared with local ingredients.

Sicily Trivia: Giardini Naxos was the first Greek colony in Sicily, founded in 734 BCE! It's possible to see the remnants of the original colony at the small archaeological park of Naxos on Via Schisò.

Side Trip

Less than a ten minute drive from the centre of Taormina is a stunning hamlet that isn't without some controversy! Castelmola is known for a few things: its spectacular views over the Ionian Sea, its charming medieval layout with a maze of narrow alleys and tiny squares, its famous almond wine and Bar Turrissi, a penis-themed bar that has been named one of the top 7 most 'peculiar' bars in the world.

Founded in 1947 but first remodelled in 1975, the owners claim the idea for a plethora of phallic symbols was inspired by their five sons. Phalluses are known to symbolise both luck and abundance! This has aroused the ire of the parish priest and some locals, who feel the hamlet has been completely rebranded as 'Penis Town'. Regardless, it's undeniable that Bar Turrisi put Castelmola firmly on the tourist map of must-sees for those with a good sense of humour.

Bar Turrisi is part bar/restaurant and part museum with a wonderful selection of Sicilian puppets and four levels overlooking both Piazza San Nicola and smoking hot Mt Etna, each with increasingly wonderful views to enjoy the local aphrodisiac, almond wine.

Incidentally, almond wine was invented in the early twentieth century in Castelmola by Don Vincenzo Blandano. Antico Caffè San Giorgio, in beautiful Piazza Sant'Antonio, still welcomes visitors who would like to try the wine (more like a liqueur) at its birthplace. The wine is often referred to locally as 'Blandanino' and is essentially a grape infusion with almonds and citrus. It has a heavy consistency. The nut flavour is not understated!

Literary fans will be interested to know that Castelmola has a connection to D.H. Lawrence's 1928 book *Lady Chatterley's Lover*. The author's wife had a torrid extramarital love affair while the two lived in Taormina for a few years. Her lover, named Mellors in the novel, was based on Peppino D'Allura, a mule keeper who lived in Castelmola and was in charge of providing transport for Mrs Lawrence on his mule when she visited friends in the countryside.

The hamlet is easy to get to, buses leave Taormina at least hourly and taxis are also available for the nine-minute trip. There is also a very steep dirt and stairs path (a former mule path) called Sentiero dei Saraceni. It's four kilometres in length, marked, but not maintained well in some parts.

Strada Provinciale 78, 95016 (Near Madonna del Carmine Church), Mascali, Catania

Scene(s) GF III:
- *Don Tomassino is shot dead in his car by the assassin Mosca of Montelepre.*

Bar Turrisi, Castelmola. Ania Mendrek, Flikr

Background

While the shooting death of Don Tomassino takes place in the street, the location of this film site is certain because the Madonna del Carmine Church can be seen in the background. The Don's death wasn't the original intention. Mosca, dressed as a priest, attempted to get inside Don Tomassino's estate to kill Michael Corleone by hitching a ride. The Don, being a gentleman, was sure to offer a lift to a priest on foot as clergy would be considered trustworthy. Tomassino recognises the famed assassin and calls him by his name 'Mosca of Montelepre'. Mosca, his plan failed, is then forced to kill him after being recognised.

Robert De Niro immerses himself in his character, Sicily. Paramount Studios

Film Facts: In the first draft of the script (written by Coppola and Puzo) for *The Godfather Part III* dated 10 May 1989, scene 101, Mosca is referred to as 'Don Mosca'. The script claims he is dressed as a 'rich landowner'. The character may have been written as a mafia 'Don' early on, thus having an elevated status, but by the final draft of the screenplay and in the film he is merely a hired assassin, working for Don Altobello.

This may account for why Don Tamassino refers to the assassin quite respectfully by both his name and birthplace, 'Mosca of Montelepre'. This could be a vestige from an earlier draft.

A character with the name Mosca appears in both *The Godfather Part II* and *The Godfather Part III*. One of Don Ciccio's two bodyguards, who hunts for young Vito after killing his mother, is also named Mosca, according to the screenplay for *Part II*.

The church itself is located on Strada Provinciale Nunziata S. Giovanni 5/SP5ii and can be seen in the background of the scene. The location of Don Tomassino's death is 300 metres away on SP78. There are no signs regarding Godfather filming.

Film Facts: Robert De Niro, the actor who played Young Vito Corleone in *The Godfather Part II*, is known to fully immerse himself when he gets a new role. His dialogue in the film is nearly entirely in Sicilian, except for a few words. The actor prepared by enrolling in Berlitz language school in addition to taking private lessons with Romano Pianti, a linguist hired by Francis Ford Coppola as a script consultant. De Niro then travelled to Taormina to practice what he had learned, living there for a few weeks and absorbing the culture. His outstanding performance won him an Oscar in 1975; he is one of only six actors so far to win an Oscar for a role mostly or solely in a foreign language.

Trinacria. Gerry Zambonini, Flikr

Sicily Trivia: Every visitor to Sicily will see Trinacria, the three-legged woman emblem. It's an ancient symbol of Sicily, adorning tiles, pottery, the flag and just about everything else. The Kingdom of Sicily, constituted in 1282, was also known as the Kingdom of Trinacria, a word derived from Greek to mean 'with three legs'. The woman in the centre is Medusa, a figure from Greek mythology known for the snakes in her hair and the ability to turn men to stone with just one look. She is a talisman against evil. The ears of wheat (or sometimes replaced with lemons) represent the fertility of the island while the three legs represent three promontories of Sicily: Cape Peloro (north-east), Cape Passero (south) and Cape Lilibeo (west).

Other Points of Interest

Teatro antico di Taormina (The Ancient Theatre of Taormina)

Built in the third century BCE but remodelled 500 years later, the ancient Greek theatre/arena is a surprisingly intact building that could possibly seat up to 10,000 spectators. The Ionian Sea, directly behind the scene (stage), provided more than a great view to those seated in the stands. The breezes helped carry the actors' voices and the

The ancient theatre of Taormina. Radek Kucharski, Flikr

musicians' music toward the crowd. Remember, this was built a long time before microphones! The round shape of the theatre also enhanced the acoustics. In its later years, it hosted popular gladiatorial games.

Nowadays, the famous Taormina Film Festival holds several of its events there. Godfather-obsessed fans who want to get in the spirit should visit in the summer when the opera *Cavalleria Rusticana* is usually on the schedule. This was the same opera that Michael Corleone's son Tony sang and performed in.

Municipal Villa, Via Bagnoli Croci
The municipal villa, the public garden of Taormina, is a lush British Victorian-inspired garden that is free to enter. The villa was originally inhabited by Lady Florence Trevelyan, a Scottish noblewoman, cousin to Queen Victoria and former mistress to Edward VII, heir to the throne of the United Kingdom. Due to the scandal, she settled in Taormina and never returned to England again. Perhaps this was the inspiration for her Victorian-style garden, complete with whimsical, novelty buildings called 'follies' that were popular in her home country, all of which can be seen today. Lady Trevelyan was also a pioneer in protecting bird habitats; she even stipulated in her will that no trees could be felled nor the land cultivated to ensure their survival. The same conditions were specified for Isola Bella, which she also owned.

Odeon, Via Timeo 31A
You'd be remiss not to check out the petite, Roman 'small theatre', built in 21 BCE, conveniently located behind the Palazzo Corvaja. It was historically used for small recitals, often poetry or music, and other events with a smaller attendance. It is commonly said that only Roman 'elites' used it but this is not archaeologically attested. Keep in mind that just because a space is smaller and more private doesn't mean its use was more exclusive. Its construction mimics the larger Greek theatre of Taormina (at that point hundreds of years old already) in that it has a stage, an orchestra and then seating in the round for visitors. The site is free to enter and none of it is off-limits to visit. It opens at 9am and closes around sunset. Small events are still held here; it's also quite magical when it's lit every evening.

Corso Umberto
Corso Umberto is the pedestrian-friendly main thoroughfare through Taormina. It follows the same route as the Consolare Valeria, the main street of the original Greco-Roman settlement. Today it is lined with upscale shops and restaurants. On either side are the city's main gates: the Arch of Porto Catania to the south and the Arch of Porto Messina to the

north. In the centre, you'll find the often photographed Piazza IX Aprile along with the clocktower, Porto Di Mezzo, which serves to delineate the Greco-Roman and the medieval parts of the city.

Odeon. Jeanne Menjoulet, Flikr

ACIREALE AND SURROUNDS

> *'But Vito is only nine. And dumb-witted. He never speaks.'*
> *'It's not his words I'm afraid of... When he is a man he'll come for revenge.'*
>
> Signora Andolini begs Don Ciccio to spare her son, *The Godfather Part II.*

Today we get to enjoy the views from Acireale but for the people of the Middle Ages, their decision to move the city from the coast to the lava steps of Timpa was a strategic one. The decision was simple: added security. The elevated location allowed the villagers to protect themselves from coastal invasions. Indeed, other villages such as Savoca and Forza d'Agrò are located at higher altitudes for this same reason. They served as good lookouts in order to prepare their defences if unwanted visitors were seen arriving. It didn't hurt that the fertile soils of Etna allowed for a large variety of produce, ranging from grapes to lemons, olives and figs. Interestingly, the presence of mulberry allowed silkworm breeding. Though not much talked about, silk production was a thriving industry in Sicily.

Today the area is still on the lookout, but for visitors... who are all welcomed with open arms and the Sicilian hospitality the locals are known for. You'll see many large, baronial estates in Acireale and the surrounding areas. Some are in a state of abandonment, others have been beautifully restored. Francis Ford Coppola clearly felt inspired by the area: three estates were filmed for *The Godfather Part II* and *Part III*.

Don Ciccio's Villa, Via Vecchia Pozzillo 46, Tonno, Acireale, Catania 95024

Scene(s) GF II:

- *Signora Andolini brings her 9-year-old son Vito to the villa to plead for his life. Don Ciccio refuses, she is shot and Vito escapes on foot.*
- *Don Vito, now an adult, returns to the villa and kills Don Ciccio as revenge for killing his father, mother and older brother; Don Tommasino is shot and wounded in the driveway.*

Background

Mystery surrounds the actual location of this atmospheric filming setting, the long-term villa of the local mafia chieftain of Corleone, Don Ciccio, in *The Godfather Part II*. Online searches usually result in erroneous information about how to find it.

Abandoned and in a state of neglect and dereliction, the villa is located in a semi-rural area not known for its tourism. Sources online, even popular maps, will list the address as 57 Via Vecchia Pozzillo. The reality is that for the classic view that we see in the movie, you'll want to look for nearby 46 Via Vecchia Pozzillo. Godfather film lovers will immediately recognise the double gates with the baronial emblems attached on both sides. Today they are painted green but in the film they are brown. Similar to when someone meets a well-known actor, the gates appear much smaller in real life than in the movie!

Currently, the villa doesn't allow visitors so looking through the gate is the only way to view the drive and the villa where young Vito was able to save his own life by running and, eventually, where Don Ciccio will lose his in an act of revenge. Only the exterior of the house was used in the film.

Don Ciccio's villa and driveway. Jonas Forth, Flikr

Don Ciccio's villa; only the exterior was filmed. Jonas Forth, Flikr

The villa, which is Sicilian Baroque in design, perfectly fulfils the description. In the screenplay, we are meant to watch the widow Andolini taking her son across a field 'leading to the ornamental gates of a Baronial estate of some forgotten Noble'. So too, the beauty of the Godfather films is in the details. Notice when Young Vito is at the estate, the cactus on the left is medium height. When Don Vito returns to kill Don Ciccio over two decades later, the cactus has grown substantially taller and the villa overall appears shabby and less maintained.

Inside Information: The neighbours of this property are friendly and used to seeing the occasional visitor searching for the property since there are no signs. The road is narrow so be sure to pull your car over as far as possible if you want to get out and take photos so as not to obstruct traffic.

Don Ciccio's villa. Jonas Forth, Flikr

Scene Analysis: In the opening scene of *The Godfather Part II*, the text tells us a few facts. We discover that Vito Andolini, later to become The Godfather, was born in Corleone, Sicily. After being insulted, the local mafia chieftain has killed Vito's father, Antonio. The mafia is then responsible for killing Vito's older brother Paolo, who swore revenge for his father. In a short time, Vito's mother will be killed whilst pleading for her only remaining son's life. The entire Andolini family, except for Vito, have been killed for an insult.

Don Ciccio represents a very old-school, traditional form of the Sicilian mafia that is still recognised as being especially brutal, even by other mafia clans around the world. Killing whole families, including children as young as two, is still routinely practised today. This is contrary to the popular myth that the mafia has ever had an honour code of sparing the lives of women or children.

It's also interesting to think about Vito's hypocrisy. He escaped to America and later chose to become a mafia boss himself, an American version of Don Ciccio, the very thing he literally ran from in Sicily.

Signora Andolini tries to defend her son. Paramount Studios

Scene Analysis: Does the revenge killing of Don Ciccio represent a pivotal moment for Don Vito? It's possible to view this scene as a moral crossing of the Rubicon, so to speak. Before this event, we witness Vito in Little Italy, aiding a neighbour in retaining her apartment and insisting on paying for oranges offered for free as a gesture of respect. In stark contrast to figures like Fanucci, Vito never resorts to intimidating tactics, such as holding a knife to someone's daughter to extort money.

In *The Godfather*, Sonny informs Michael that everything is strictly business, and nothing is personal, even after the attempted assassination of their father. Clearly, Don Vito didn't share this perspective. While it's understandable that he harbours resentment towards Don Ciccio for the 1901 massacre of his family, the elderly Ciccio no longer posed a threat. In reality, Vito would likely have made the same brutal decision as Ciccio did. This act of vengeance is intensely personal.

The idea that the violence orchestrated by the Corleone family is all business is a blatant justification, but only in their minds, for the acts that they committed.

Don Vito murders Don Ciccio. Paramount Studios

> **Film Facts:** 'Ciccio' is the Sicilian diminutive for 'Francesco'. In the screenplay, Don Ciccio is referred to as Don Francesco and is described as having an 'enormous belly'. In Italian, 'Ciccio' is a nonoffensive nickname meaning 'chubby'.

Vito looks for Strollo, from a deleted scene.
Paramount Studios

Did You Know?

When travelling around Sicily and Italy itself it is common to see derelict houses and even whole villages that have been abandoned. There are several reasons for this. Sometimes it can be accounted for because the local industry has been made obsolete; other times the infrastructure, including roads, makes living there inconvenient for work. The remaining residents move or die off, dwindling populations leaving ghost villages in their wake.

Local governments of towns such as Sambuca and Gangi have come up with an innovative way to survive: they sell dilapidated houses for the symbolic sum of one Euro. The buyer is then required to submit a deposit and agree to renovate the property, usually within three years. The average costs of these renovations are often in the six-figure range and you will need patience to deal with local contractors in the newly booming building market. Of course, you'll also need to pay taxes!

Film Facts: Don Ciccio isn't the only person in Sicily that Vito seeks revenge against when he returns with his family. In two deleted scenes, Vito also kills Mosca and Strollo, Don Ciccio's bodyguards. Both of these men looked for Vito extensively throughout Corleone after he managed to escape death at the villa. They were also responsible for killing his mother.

Villa La Limonaia, Via Carico 149, Acireale, Catania

Scene(s) GF III:
- Vincent Mancini meets with Don Altobello at his home and kisses his hand on the terrace.
- Don Altobello introduces Vincent to Don Lucchessi in the courtyard.

Background

The beautiful, pink Neoclassical villa was built for a nobleman during the first half of the eighteenth century and has undergone dramatic renovations since. The name means 'lemon house' in Italian and it serves as Don Altobello's Sicilian home in *The Godfather Part III*. Currently, it is used for events.

Fans will remember Don Altobello's backstory. He and Don Vito were very

old family friends; Altobello was even chosen to be Connie's (religious) godfather just after her birth and would have been present at her baptism. This is an important role in the Catholic faith and Don Vito would have only given it to a man that he trusted to be a spiritual parent to his child. In *The Godfather Part III*, we see Altobello at the Atlantic City Commission meeting, where the heads of the predominate mafia families had gathered to meet. Joey Zasa, an enemy of the Corleone family, becomes emotional and storms out of the room. Don Altobello follows him, claiming he wants to calm Zasa down. He doesn't return. The conference room doors are then locked with handcuffs, trapping the other men inside. Infamously, a helicopter attack on the room leaves the heads of the families dead, though Michael Corleone, his nephew Vincent Mancini and his long-term bodyguard Al Neri all manage to escape.

Michael was suspicious of Altobello's role in orchestrating the Atlantic City massacre. Later in the film, whilst in Sicily, Michael instructs Vincent to visit Don Altobello at his home, to falsely pledge his allegiance to him and to find out the truth. It is at Villa La Limonaia, on the terrace, that Vincent talks with Altobello and is then later introduced to his co-conspirator Don Lucchessi.

Villa La Limonaia. Villa La Limonaia

The terrace of Villa La Limonaia. Villa La Limonaia

Vincent Mancini meets Don Altobello at Villa La Limonaia. Paramount Studios

'Finance is a gun. Politics is knowing when to pull the ...trigger.'
Don Lucchessi, *The Godfather Part III.*

Etna Lemons: The Mt Etna volcano provides a fertile landscape most famously for wine grapes but for also the equally delicious Limone dell'Etna. These lemons, having been cultivated in the Etna soil and subject to the coastal climate of the Ionian Sea, are so unique that they have been granted an official protected agricultural status of 'IGP'. This designation lets the consumer know they are getting an authentic product, grown in volcanic soil and with the characteristics that an Etna lemon should have. Look for that mark (IGP) on the label if you wish to try one. Scientific research has demonstrated that these lemons produce up to 30 per cent more juice and essential oils in their peel. They are harvested four times a year, with the autumn and summer lemons being light or dark green in colour and the others, yellow. From lemon seltzer water to liquors, to honey and essential oils, you'll see plenty of products for sale in Acireale and the surrounding area that incorporate the Etna lemon.

Film Facts: In a previous draft of *The Godfather Part III*, written by Mario Puzo and Francis Ford Coppola, Don Altobello is involved in a different scheme very reminiscent of the real-life 1957 Apalachin meeting. During that meeting, over a hundred mafia bosses from the USA, Italy and even Cuba met at an upstate New York mansion to discuss mafia business and to divide up control in their business interests. The local police became suspicious, raided the house and detained more than sixty underworld mob bosses. All of these men were initially given prison sentences.

In the draft, we see a similar scene. The heads of the family meet, not in Atlantic City, but at Don Altobello's upstate New York home and it is he himself who tips off police to raid his home. He is not detained. Instead of death by helicopter, Altobello gathers power for himself by using law enforcement to rid himself of the other heads of the families.

It's unknown exactly why this scene was rewritten for the film but there are a few clues. The director has commented that he needed to both dramatically 'wipe out' twenty people in a way that hadn't really been done before and also live up to the violence in the first two Godfather films. This is how the helicopter idea came about. The fact that Joey Zasa's character was based on the real-life John Gotti, a mobster known for his flashiness, also inspired the use of a helicopter. Lastly, the draft put the Tom Hagen character front and centre. However, when the actor Robert Duvall did not reprise his role in the story due to a salary dispute, it needed to be rewritten to exclude his character.

Castello Scammacca di Acireale (also known as Castello Pennisi di Floristella), Piazza Agostino Pennisi, 11, Acireale, Catania

Scene(s) GF III:
- Calo arrives at Don Lucchessi's house.
- Calo meets with and kills Don Lucchessi in his office.

Background

Neogothic in design and built in 1882, this eclectic building was constructed as a home for the art collection of Baron Agostino Pennisi of Floristella. Five generations of the family have lived there since. It made worldwide news when in 2020 the castle was put on the real estate market for 6.8 million Euros. For those that can afford *La Dolce Vita*, it has twenty-two bedrooms

Castello Scammacca. GiovanniPen, WikiCommons

and is set on 2.1 acres. As of 2023, it has been taken off the market. Besides the good fortune of being filmed in *The Godfather Part III*, it survived the devastating earthquake of 1908 plus the Allied bombing of Acireale during World War II.

The castle served as Don Lucchessi's house in the scenes. The exterior and a few rooms on the first floor were filmed. A private residence, it is not open to visitors currently though locals speculate it will be used for commercial purposes if it sells. This home is a private residence and does not accept visitors.

It was Baron Pennisi himself who befriended Francis Ford Coppola in the 1970s when he came to Sicily to scout locations for *The Godfather*. He is credited with suggesting both Savoca and Forza d'Agrò as filming locations when Coppola realised that the real-life town of Corleone wouldn't suit his purposes.

'The past is always having a war with the future.'

Francis Ford Coppola, 2020, reflecting on the different artistic direction he decided to take when making *The Godfather Part III*.

Sicily Trivia: Everywhere you go in Sicily you are sure to find arancini! Sicilian arancini are, essentially, a deep-fried rice ball stuffed with different ingredients. They are called 'arancine' in Palermo and West Sicily, but in Catania and East Sicily they are referred to as 'arancini'. The name derives from the Italian word for 'orange' due to its shape and saffron colour. Their origins go way back. It's believed they were brought by the Arabs, who dominated Sicily from 827 until 1091, though the breading and tomato additions came later. The most popular are those with meat sauce but Catania has its very own called 'alla catanese' which includes aubergine as an ingredient. Fierce competition exists among the cities for who makes the best and everyone has an opinion!

Arancini. stu_spivack, iStock

Annual Carnival of Acireale, February during Carnival Season
The Carnival of Acireale is considered the most famous and well-attended in all of Sicily. It has recently been described as one of the top ten most beautiful in Europe. Generally lasting about three weeks, it's also one of the oldest. Records show it dates back to at least 1594. Folk bands from all over Italy participate in this prelude to Catholic Lent. The Carnival is so popular that a shorter version is repeated in August, the tourist season, with the floats on display on the main avenues and in the squares.

Historically, Carnival gave ordinary citizens the freedom to make jokes about both the elites in power and to mock the clergy. Any other time of the year expressing your opinion could end in a fine, prison or much worse. There are two types of floats to enjoy: the allegorical (satirical) floats as well as the floats embellished with flowers. Not only are politicians satirised. Recent floats have included popular figures such as Steve Jobs.

There are several famous masks as well. The Abbatazzu wear large white wigs and frilly clothes, they are meant to mock the clergy. In a similar vein, the Baruni mocks the noble classes. Modern-day, this is all very light-hearted. It is great fun for everyone, including your pets, who are allowed to participate in the parade on a day designated as 'Carnevanimale'.

The end of the festivities is marked by the burning at the stake of the 'Re Carnevale' (King Carnival).

For those who are especially interested, the Carnival Museum is located in the Piazza del Turismo on Via Ruggero Settimo 11 and open all year round.

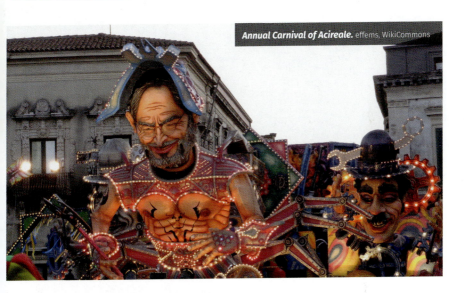

Annual Carnival of Acireale. effems, WikiCommons

Stazione FS di Sparagogna (Sparagogna Railway Station), Regalbuto, Enna 94017

Scene(s) GF II:
- Don Vito and his family arrive in Corleone.
- Don Vito and his family leave Corleone by train, Michael (a toddler) waves from the window at Don Tommassino and others on the platform.

Background

A forty-five-minute drive outside of the city of Catania will take you to a railway station that anyone familiar with the Godfather films will recognise. No longer in use, the Sparagogna Railway Station served as the Corleone railway station for the newly prosperous Don Vito and his family's return in the 1920s. Arrangements had been made with the Italian state railroad (*Ferrovie dello Stato*) to close off the tracks between Catania and Palermo to film the scenes.

Sparagogna Railway Station, Enna. Paramount Studios

The scene with Vito and his son Michael waving from the train window is shown twice in *The Godfather Part II*. The second time is during the final scene of the film: we see Michael sitting alone in a chair outdoors where he has a brief flashback of himself, as a child, waving from the train. Perhaps it was one of his earliest memories? He clearly looks reflective sitting there. In 1975, Francis Ford Coppola remarked about the ending: 'There's no doubt that, by the end of this picture, Michael Corleone, having beaten everyone, is sitting there alone, a living corpse.' The contrast between a scene of a waving, innocent child in sunny Sicily and Michael, sitting alone and surrounded by dead leaves at Lake Tahoe, beautifully lets the viewer know how things have turned out for him. Coppola has remarked many times that he had no intention of ever making a Part III so that last scene, for the time being at least, was considered to be the end of Michael's story.

Note that this station is different from the 'Bagheria' station Kay arrives at in *The Godfather Part III*. The real-life location for that scene is in Taormina.

> **Film Facts:** The Italian state showed *The Godfather* and *The Godfather Part II* back to back in the later part of the 1970s. Record television audiences left the Sicilian streets so deserted that many cafes and restaurants chose to close.

Other Points of Interest

Piazza Duomo, Acireale
The main square of Acireale has twin churches, one of which has a name you may remember. The first is the seventeenth-century Maria Santissima Annunziata, which has a similar name to the cathedral in Forza d'Agrò used extensively throughout the Trilogy. Don't get confused, no scenes were filmed here in the Piazza Duomo.

> **Inside Information:** If you decide to visit the Piazza Duomo and would also like to try some of the best arancini in the entire Catania province, the casual eatery Il Rosticcere, Corso Savoia 50, is a short three-minute walk away. Arancini and everything else is available to eat in or to take away.

Mt Etna Cable Car, Piazzale Funivia, 95030 Nicolosi, Catania
It's not uncommon to meet visitors to Acireale who have made arrangements to trek up 'Mother Etna' as the locals say. However, there is an alternative

Mt Etna cable car. John Button, Flikr

way to see it. Once parked at Refugio Sapienza, a cable car (*Funivia dell'Etna*) is available that ascends to 840 metres (2,750 feet). Once you have gotten that far, you have the option to walk or take a bus further up. Since the Godfather films were set in the town of Corleone, the volcano is never seen in the films.

'All that nature has of great, all it has of pleasant, all it has of terrible, can be compared to Etna, and Etna cannot be compared to anything.'
French artist and writer Dominique Vivant Denon, *Voyage in Lower and Upper Egypt during the campaigns of General Bonaparte.*

Is it dangerous to stay near Mt Etna?

Since pre-history, people have learned to co-exist with the volcano they often call 'Mother Etna'. The tallest and largest active volcano in Europe, with four central craters including one that never stops spewing smoke, it's a force of nature that transforms the landscape, sometimes dramatically. If you find yourself in Catania, you'll find a painting by Giacinto Platania hanging in the Cathedral of Catania that recounts the catastrophic 1669 lava eruption. On the other hand, the lava flows have created a fertile and extremely productive soil, providing locals with world-famous citrus, wine, olives and other agricultural products. Due to this, 20 percent of Sicilians live on its slopes.

So is it safe to visit?

Overall Etna has been described as a safe volcano. The main reason for this is because it is so tall. The craters are located far from towns. Additionally, because the lava flow is slow and sticky, it tends to cool and solidify near the crater. In fact, Mt Etna will visually change its shape, especially during periods of heavy activity. In 2021 it grew by 30 metres in the space of six months. Age helps too, older volcanoes tend to be less restless. The National Institute of Geophysics and Volcanology (INGV) also has a facility in nearby Catania that provides monitoring and forecasting. The INGV look at things like seismic activity and sulphur dioxide increases. They work in collaboration with the Civil Protection authorities, who have historically built earthen barriers if a lava flow gets a little too close for comfort to a village or infrastructure. Even then, there is no threat to human life since the lava flows slowly. Incredibly, you are still able to hike Mt Etna even while it is erupting. Occasionally, Catania Airport does need to be closed due to ash, an annoyance but not a dangerous one.

Mt Etna, covered in snow. Andrea, Flikr

Museo Del Cinema, Piazzale Rocco Chinnici, 95129 Catania

It takes about twenty-five minutes by car to get to the Museo Del Cinema (Museum of Cinema) from Acireale but for cinema fans, it is worth it. This quirky, charming and well-designed museum has several life-sized reconstructed sets depicting scenes from various movies filmed in Sicily. It also includes movie artefacts and posters, including some Godfather memorabilia and a Godfather-inspired set. The history of cinema and its evolution in Italy are also recounted, all in an immersive way. It isn't well advertised. Currently, it only costs 4 euros to enter.

PALERMO AND SURROUNDS

'Palermo was lovely. The most beautifully situated town in the world – it dreams away its life in the Conca d'Oro, the exquisite valley that lies between two seas. The lemon groves and the orange gardens were entirely perfect.'
Oscar Wilde, 1900.

A few things come to mind when thinking of Palermo, the capital city of Sicily: its mishmash of architectural styles, chaotic traffic, gritty streets and the famous outdoor market La Vucciria that becomes a street party every night. Graffiti occupies every space. It was bombed more than seventy times during World War II, which doesn't aid its physical appearance since many of the ruins were never rebuilt. Due to its geographic location and natural harbour, it is also considered to be the most conquered city in the world. The Phoenicians, Greeks, Romans, Arabs, Normans, Spanish and more all left their cultural mark both when colonising the city and when leaving it. The term 'urban melting pot' comes to mind. A less savoury review called it 'decaying' and with 'rotting elegance'. Some people describe the vibe as peculiar. The city has a secretive feel about it, a lot goes unspoken.

Mentally, many visitors associate Palermo with the mafia. Unfortunately, there's some truth in this assumption. In 1992, the anti-mafia judges Giovanni Falcone and Paolo Borsellino were both assassinated by bombs (along with family members, bodyguards and police); neither man would back down from attempting to rid Sicily of Cosa Nostra, the Sicilian mafia. Both magistrates were sacrificed for their cause. They remain heroes to this day. Their names can be seen on buildings, memorials and even the airport.

Yet pockets of art and beauty exist and there are Godfather filming sites to visit along with several other points of interest, several of which feature in mafia history. The food is superb, to put it mildly. Restaurants, shops and other commercial establishments have formally banded together in refusing to pay extortion money to the mob; ethical tourism now exists. A new day is dawning for this 'beautifully situated' city. Courageous anti-mafia groups like Adiopizzo are picking up where Falcone, Borsellino and other patriots left off. Cosa Nostra's days are waning, its grip is weakening. Palermo is attracting more visitors than ever before and hoping to shed its uninviting stereotype.

Teatro Massimo Vittorio Emanuele, Piazza Verde, Palermo, Commune di Palermo

Scene(s) GF III:
- Anthony 'Tony' Corleone makes his operatic debut at the theatre, his family and concert goers arrive on the steps outside.
- Mary Corleone is shot to death on the exterior steps.

Background

Only the exterior of the Teatro Massimo was filmed for *The Godfather Part III*. The theatre was undergoing major renovations for safety regulations (for a mind-boggling twenty-three years) and therefore any scenes you see 'inside the opera house' were instead filmed on a replica soundstage at Cinecittà Studios in Rome. The real-life interior of the theatre looks nearly identical to the one seen in the film. Guided tours are available in English and they will even let you sit in the Royal Box that the Corleones supposedly occupied. It's worth a visit, just understand that the theatre was never filmed inside!

Neoclassical in design and highly reminiscent of a Greek temple, it's

Teatro Massimo at night.
Massimiliano Serrago, Addiopizzo

known for its perfect acoustics due to its thick stone walls and structural design. The name aptly translates to 'maximum theatre'. It is the largest theatre in Italy and one of the largest in Europe. Fans will immediately recognise the two large bronze lion statues next to the stairway entrance.

Today, more than 100 operas and other performances are available to see year-round. The exterior stairs are very much at the heart of Palermo, attracting families eating gelato, local teenagers meeting up and of course Godfather aficionados as well.

Cavalleria Rusticana, the opera
Tony Corleone's operatic debut in Mascagni's *Cavalleria Rusticana* in *The Godfather Part III* feels like a mere background to the murders taking place in the opera house alongside the tension of whether Michael Corleone will be assassinated. However, the opera, set in a nineteenth-century Sicilian village, is an apt choice for the film.

The story involves Turiddu, who has returned from military duty and finds himself involved in a love triangle with two women. The husband of one of his lovers swears a vendetta and challenges Turiddu to a duel. In Sicilian tradition, the two men embrace and Turiddu bites the man's ear, drawing blood. This signifies a fight to the death. Does that look familiar? The scene cuts to Vincent Mancini, laughing, which should give a hint. Suddenly overwhelmed with guilt, Turiddu realises how badly he has hurt his lovers, one lover's husband, and has even disgraced his own mother. Moments later, a woman cries out that Turiddu has been killed.

Regret, vendettas, brutality and death are all major themes in the Godfather films. This opera was chosen because it represents a sort of rural origin story for both Don Vito and Don Michael, that brutal revenge originates in their ancestry.

Film Facts: In a previous draft version of the script, the opera house scenes are significantly less dramatic. Tony's operatic debut goes perfectly. The next day, Michael Corleone and his family are ascending the stairs of a Palermo cathedral to attend mass. Mosca, the assassin, steps from the waiting crowd and shoots and kills Michael Corleone, not his daughter Mary.

The Corleones attend the opera. Paramount Studios

Film Facts: *The Godfather* opened in Palermo on 12 October 1972. The film was dubbed in the Sicilian language. According to reports, the language was a bit spicier than the English language version and came across as more forceful and with less nuance. A former Palermo District Attorney was said to have reacted negatively after seeing it, claiming it glorified the wrong people.

'Just as in the story, it was Sofia that they [the media] shot the bullets at, but they were really shooting them at me… That is ultimately really what the film was about: that there is no worse way to pay for your sins than to have your children be included in the punishment.'

Francis Ford Coppola's comments for *The Godfather Part III*, regarding the casting of his often criticised daughter Sophia Coppola for the role of Mary and his decision for Mary to be killed at the end of the film instead of her father, Michael Corleone.

> **Inside Information:** Arguably, the best pizza to be had in Palermo is very close to the opera house. The casual, modern restaurant Biga Genio e Farina, Via Maqueda 284-286, is a mere four-minute walk away. Eat in or takeaway, their incredible Sicilian-style pizzas are available by the (large) slice for three to four Euros each. They are famous for their Margherita di Biga, using only Sicilian ingredients and also for their sumptuous dough. If you are in Palermo for more than a day, don't be surprised to find yourself stopping here more than once. Open 11am until midnight every day.

Did You Know?

The hit HBO series *The White Lotus* Season 2 takes place in Sicily. A few of the characters are Godfather fans (how could you not be?) and, in the show, they visit several Godfather filming locations. Viewers will see that the Teatro Massimo was filmed for episode five, where a group arrive to see Puccini's *Madame Butterfly*.

Villa Malfitano Whitaker, Via Dante Alighieri 167, Palermo, Commune di Palermo

Scene(s) GF III:

- *Michael Corleone, his former wife Kay and their children arrive at and stay at this villa while in Palermo.*
- *A party is held to honour Anthony Corleone's operatic debut at which he sings.*
- *Vincent and Mary kiss in an upstairs bedroom.*
- *Michael Corleone, while being shaved, asks Vincent to arrange a meeting with Don Altobello.*
- *Mary Corleone looks at a photo album with pictures from Michael and Apollonia's wedding.*
- *Michael and Connie sit on a porch, Connie injects insulin for Michael and they discuss their brother Fredo's death.*
- *Vincent Corleone plays billiards with the twins.*
- *Kay exits the house and enters a car only to find that Michael is the driver.*
- *In the billiards room, Connie makes Vincent swear revenge if anything should happen to her brother Michael.*

Background

Villa Malfitano Whitaker has the distinction of having been filmed externally as well as internally for numerous scenes in *The Godfather Part III*. Interestingly, they do nothing to promote this about themselves, there are no signs, and there is no mention of the film at all. Instead, the Whitaker Foundation claims that the villa aims to promote 'the study and knowledge of the Phoenician-Punic civilisation in the Mediterranean.'

Villa Malfitano was built in 1886 by the Sicilian-English Joseph Whitaker and is set on a park of seven hectares. It includes several specimens of exotic and rare plants. Whitaker, whose family came from West Yorkshire, made his fortune through the inheritance of a Marsala wine business. He was an extremely well-published ornithologist, his speciality being the birds of Tunisia. Later in life, he became interested in archaeology. He purchased the island of Motya (on the west coast of Sicily) and excavated the site of an eighth-century BCE Phoenician town. This excavation can still be visited today. The villa serves as a museum containing the family's collection of artwork, artefacts, and antiques.

Both the billiards room and the reception room where a party was held in Anthony Corleone's honour look exactly as they did in the film. The piano that Anthony sat at is still

Al Pacino at Villa Malfitano. Paramount Studios

Piano at Villa Malfitano. Author's Collection

in the same location. The external scenes were filmed at the back of the house, not the front. Look for the lion statues flanking a columnated porch, reminiscent of a Greek temple. It's interesting to note that two lion sculptures flank the Teatro Massimo, which also resembles a Greek temple. The villa's garden and small fountain can be seen in the background of the scene between Michael and his sister Connie, on a porch, where they discuss their brother Fredo's death.

Billiards room, Villa Malfitano. Author's Collection

In the mid-1990s the Villa was included in the adopt-a-monument programme. Students from the city were matched up with cultural monuments around the city that were neglected or hidden from view and encouraged to create tours for people to visit. The aim was to increase the sense of cultural ownership and responsibility often lacking in mafia dominated communities.

Scene Analysis: Did Connie know that her brother Michael ordered the deaths of both her husband Carlo (as seen in *The Godfather*) and their brother Fredo (as seen in *The Godfather Part II*)? This question comes up for debate often among Godfather fans, who are divided.

There are a few things to consider. On the porch scene, where Connie helpfully administers insulin to Michael, he tells her that he made a confession with a priest earlier that day. Connie is surprised by this and remarks how unlike him it is to confess his sins to 'a stranger'. She immediately says 'Michael, you know, sometimes I think of poor Fredo, drowned. It was God's will. It was a terrible accident. But it's finished.' This unusual response after Michael tells her he confessed his sins may have been Connie's way of letting her brother know she forgives him for the choices he had to make.

In a previous draft of the film, dated May 1989 and written by Coppola and Puzo, Connie directly admits to Michael that she knew he ordered Carlo's death as well as Fredo's. She says 'I forgive you. It took so many years but I forgive you now.' She then blames herself for marrying Carlo in the first place saying 'I was used so that they could kill Sonny.' Connie further implores Michael 'You can't let your guilt weaken us... You did terrible things, I know. But I forgive you my husband, I forgive you Fredo.' Coppola and Puzo clearly knew that Connie wasn't naïve about the situation. In a later draft, from November 1989, Connie recites a similar dialogue.

Furthermore, the rest of the family knew that Michael killed his brother. Kay, while at the party celebrating the honour bestowed on Michael from the church, directly tells Michael that their son Tony knows he committed fratricide. In a later scene, Mary Corleone asks Vincent bluntly if her father killed his own brother. Vincent doesn't seem surprised by the question. It's a curiosity how the family even discovered the truth about Fredo's murder; this is never shown in the films.

In light of all of this, it is reasonable to assume Connie was aware that Michael ordered the death of Carlo and Fredo even if she didn't directly say so. Furthermore, Connie has no issue with killing when she feels it is justified. She poisons her own godfather later in the film. Though Don Altobello wasn't a blood relation, he would have been considered part of her spiritual family, from a Catholic viewpoint.

Scene Analysis: During Anthony's private performance at the party hosted by his father, the viewer is shown a flashback of Michael and Apollonia's wedding, more than thirty years prior. Not so subtly, Michael then glances at his own daughter Mary. It is easy to see why he is so opposed to her relationship with Vincent Mancini, now that Vincent is on course to become the Godfather of the family. Regardless, history repeats itself. Just as Apollonia was killed by a bomb meant to kill her husband, Mary loses her life to a bullet meant to kill her father.

Michael and Apollonia. Paramount Studios

Film Facts: When *The Godfather Part III* was shown in Palermo, six carabinieri (Italian military police) with machine guns were stationed outside of the Cinema Nazionale in the heart of Palermo. The government was concerned that real-life mafiosi may cause problems at the film's opening.

A few weeks prior, 41 convicted mafia bosses, murderers and drug kingpins had been released from jail, benefitting from a legal loophole. They were jailed again soon after but Sicilians were preparing themselves for an uptick in violence. The first two Godfather movies were well-received in Sicily. The third, not so much. Afterwards, Sicilians complained that the character of Michael asks for the audience's sympathy. They were understandably dismissive of Michael Corleone's redemptive arc as realistic in light of the hundreds of annual murders that were being committed by the mafia, often of hapless bystanders.

Did You Know?

Those with an interest in mafia history should stop by the glamorous Belle Epoque Grand Hotel et des Palmes in Palermo on Via Roma 398. The same family that owns Villa Malfitano also constructed this hotel as a private residence; it was converted in 1907 into a commercial establishment and has remained a hotel ever since.

The infamous 1957 Palermo Mafia Summit was held at the hotel, lasting four days between 12-16 October. In some circles, this is known as the 'heroin summit'. Notable American and Sicilian mafioso such as Joe Bonanno, Lucky Luciano, Salvatore 'Little Bird' Greco, Giuseppe Genco Russo and Tommaso Buscetta met to determine how and who would distribute French-produced ('French Connection') heroin within the American market.

This summit served to establish the American Bonnano crime family in the heroin trade. It also reforged relationships between the Sicilian Cosa Nostra and their American criminal counterparts, especially since, historically, the Sicilians were not major players in the global drug trade up until this point. This wasn't due to any mythological 'honour code' of not selling drugs, rather it was because they lacked distribution channels. The Palermo Mafia Summit changed that. The connection between the American and Sicilian mob became so close that charter flights between Palermo and New York City increased in number and the airport had to be updated. New bank branches opened all over the city.

No first-hand accounts exist, though the Sicilian police did observe the gatherings and reported on them.

Grand Hotel des Palmes, early twentieth century. Di Benedetto, E., Biblioteca Comunale Palermo

The mafia, naturally, denies that the summit even took place. Eight years later, Palermo prosecutors indicted seventeen of the participants, both Sicilian and American. The Court of Palermo dismissed the charges a year later.

Interestingly, it should be noted that only a month later, on 14 November 1957, the Apalachin mafia summit in upstate New York was held. It's believed that part of the agenda of this meeting was to discuss the outcome of the Sicilian summit and to further divide narcotics trafficking amongst the American mafia families. This meeting was raided and several figures that had been present the month prior in Sicily were arrested.

The drug trade is spoken about extensively in the Godfather films. In the first film, we see Don Vito adamant that he would never get involved in the drug business. Yet during the meeting with the Five Families, he concedes. Under seemingly chivalrous conditions he agrees to participate, namely that drugs cannot be sold to children and that sales should be kept within black neighbourhoods. In reality, there is no evidence that the real-life summit participants had any qualms about selling heroin to whoever had the cash to purchase it, regardless of their age or race. The introduction of heroin on a mass scale would have repercussions in the United States for decades thereafter.

The famed Lucky Luciano was a regular visitor to the hotel. However, the Grand Hotel et des Palmes is keener to promote that the composer Richard Wagner spent a year writing his masterpiece *Parsifal* there, so inspired he was by the surroundings, that the Presidential Suite is named for him.

Regardless, the hotel is such a part of mafia and artistic history that entire books have been written about it.

Cannoli: A History

No visit to Sicily would be complete without trying the famous 'cannolo' pastry ('cannoli' being the plural). So good are they that even Clemenza couldn't help but retrieve them from his car that had become a murder scene just moments before.

Modern cannoli are almost certainly an Arab invention, dating to between 827 and 1091 CE. In its simplest form, cannoli are a deep-fried crust filled with sugar-sweetened, fresh ricotta cheese derived from sheep's milk. The word comes to us from the word 'canna', in this case meaning a sugar cane stalk. Hundreds of years ago, the dough would be rolled out in a circle and wrapped around the sugar cane reed, giving it a tubular shape. Originally, they were eaten in the Spring because the sheep produce more milk when their pastures turn green with the season. Even today Spring is considered the best time to purchase ricotta.

From here the history gets a little murky. Some say that the pastry is of Roman origin. That isn't impossible but while Romans knew about sugar cane they preferred to sweeten their foods with honey. Sugar was a medicine, not a food. Cicero, the Roman orator, mentions eating them when he was Quaestor in Sicily in 75 BCE. The Arabs may have elaborated on a Roman recipe, using sugar, a commodity to which the Moors were very accustomed to using but little known in Sicily until the island came under Arab domination.

The most popular and saucier legend is that they originated in Caltanissetta, created by the female harem of an Arab prince. The bored women idled away in the kitchen, baking pastries in a shape that served as a tribute to his manhood. Supposedly. Others claim that nuns crafted the dessert for Carnevale, the celebration right before Lent. The reality is likely a mix of the two. Nuns would have crafted the dessert for Carnevale and they may have become associated as a phallic symbol by festival goers. It doesn't take much imagination for people to make that association.

The ideal cannolo should have a thin crust but often you will find them served with a thicker, crunchier crust since these are easier to fry and break less easily. The filling, cold but not frozen, should be inserted directly before serving. Sometimes you will come across cannoli lined with chocolate on the inside as a barrier between the crust and ricotta, to reduce the possibility of sogginess. This isn't ideal since, in reality, the pastries are being filled hours or maybe days in advance for the convenience of the baker. The true cannolo connoisseur will turn their nose up at this. But then again, who doesn't like chocolate? You may also see pistachio or chocolate chips sprinkled on top; the purists must again deny themselves.

There is no standard size. You can find them ranging from bite sized to the famed cannoli of Piana degli Albanesi, which are the size of your hand. Piana is home to Marco Cuccio, nicknamed 'The King of Cannoli'; he is considered to be the best cannoli maker in the world. When interviewed, he felt that nuns were the first to produce them. His restaurant 'La Casa del Cannolo' is popular with pastry enthusiasts.

As you may recall, Connie Corleone managed to weaponise some cannoli with poison once it was determined that Don Altobello was involved in the plot to kill her brother.

Caravaggio's Painting *Nativity with St. Francis and St. Lawrence*: A Mafia Art Heist

One of the most significant art thefts in human history took place in Palermo at the hands of the Sicilian mafia, never to be found again.

Caravaggio, the painter whose name is instantly recognisable the world over, has around 100 pieces of known art attributed to him currently. His 1609 painting of the nativity scene of Jesus, completed a year before his death, illustrates his mastery of chiaroscuro, the interplay of light and dark for dramatic effect. It hung in Palermo's Oratory of St Lawrence until it was viciously cut from its frame and stolen in 1969. Its whereabouts are still unknown. Investigators agree that Cosa Nostra was involved.

Clues to its fate can be gleaned from the accounts of various mafia informants. One informant claimed that a private individual commissioned him to steal it, only to cry when seeing how damaged it was during the theft and refusing to pay. Another informant claims it was passed from mob boss to mob boss, eventually ending up in the barn of a family where it was gnawed on by rats and then burned. Most absurd, one man claims it was used as a floor mat by the ruthless chief of the Sicilian mafia, Salvatore Riina. Given the occupation of the informants, it is difficult to determine the truth without any evidence. In 2015, a replica was made and can be seen in the Oratory today.

The United States FBI has listed this theft among their 'Top Ten Art Crimes'. This act of cultural genocide is still an open case.

Palermo No Mafia Walking Tour (Addiopizzo Travel)
This three hour walking tour is a must-do for anyone with an interest in the impact of the mafia on Sicily and its culture. Courageously organised and presented by members of a grassroots movement that works to resist the mafia, 'pizzo' refers to the extortion money demanded from nearly all

Oratory of St Lawrence. Salvo Loiacono, WikiCommons

Addiopizzo logo as seen in shop windows. Andrea Brandino, Addiopizzo

businesses in Sicily. Brave businesses that sign up to the Addiopizzo movement refuse to pay the mafia even under threats of property damage and the personal safety of themselves and their families. Look for the orange Addiopizzo ('goodbye, pizzo') sticker in their shop windows.

We see numerous examples in the Godfather films of businesses being forced to pay the pizzo, most heartbreakingly when Don Fanucci pays a visit to Abbandando's grocery store and demands money and a job for his nephew. Young Vito loses his job as a grocery clerk as a result. In another scene, Don Fanucci doesn't hesitate to hold a knife against the face of a young singer in an attempt to get her father to pay up. Later, we also see Fanucci ask Vito, Clemenza and Tessio to wet his beak for merchandise they have stolen and sold; this leads to his murder. The term 'pizzo' is derived from the Sicilian word 'pizzu', which means 'beak'.

These scenarios are still very much a reality in Sicily. More than half of businesses on the island admit to currently paying the criminal toll, down from 80 per cent in the 1990s. Highlights of the tour include a stop at the seventy-meter-long Wall of Legality, painted with the faces of mafia victims plus a stop at the Palermo Cathedral, where the relationship between the Church and mafia is discussed.

Addiopizzo also operates a travel company called Addiopizzo Travel; all of the businesses patronised on their itineraries have refused to pay extortion money.

Inside Information: The historic restaurant L'Antica Focacceria S. Francesco, Via Alessandro Paternostro, 58, is a founding member of the Addiopizzo movement. Not only that, but they purchase their ingredients from the association Libero Terra. This group reuses the lands confiscated from the mafia, giving them back to farmers. The restaurant is known for its traditional Sicilian street food. You can enjoy an *arancina al ragu* or any of their vegetarian offerings knowing your money isn't going directly into the pockets of the mafia.

Templo de Segesta (Temple of Segesta), Contrado Barbaro, Calatafimi, Trapani

Scenes(s) GF III:
- *The Corleones and their entourage drive past the Temple of Segesta, referred to as 'Bagheria' in the film.*

Temple of Segesta. Tiberio Frascari, Flikr

Background

Our first introduction to Sicily in *The Godfather Part III* shows the three-car entourage of the Corleone family driving past the Greek Temple of Segesta. The text at the bottom of the screen refers to the area as 'Bagheria'. This Doric temple was built at the end of the fifth century BCE, on a hill with commanding views of the valley below and is only about an hour from Palermo. It has no roof, and both the temple and the nearby ancient theatre were never completed. Regardless, it is remarkably intact and beautifully sets the scene. The Corleones have returned to an ancient land, the old world with its ancient customs. The columned 'Greek temple' theme is evident throughout *The Godfather Part III*, and we see it again at Teatro Massimo and also at Villa Malfitano.

Chiesa di Sant'Orsola (Church of Saint Ursula), Via Addolorata near Porta Spada, Erice, Trapani

Scenes(s) GF III:
- *The exterior of the convent that Don Tommasino arrives by car to join Michael Corleone and Cardinal Lamberto.*

Background

In this scene we see Don Tommasino arriving by car outside of the church. Only the exterior of St Ursula's was filmed, the interior scenes were filmed in Viterbo, mainland Italy, at the Church of Santa Maria Della Quercia.

The Don is being lifted gently from a car and his bodyguards place him in his wheelchair. He joins Michael Corleone and Cardinal Lamberto inside, where Michael later makes a confession to the priest that he killed his own brother. It's a very short scene.

It's easy to see why the director Francis Ford Coppola decided to film this church; he certainly had a lot to choose from. It's twin bells and Phoenician walls (which fortified the city in ancient times) lend a lot of texture and visual appeal.

Erice, like Savoca, has been named as one of the most beautiful villages in Italy. Its nickname is 'the city of a hundred churches' though that number is a bit of an exaggeration. Virgil, in his epic poem the Aeneid, mentions the town by its original Greek name (Eryx). It's located about ninety minutes by car from Palermo and is a popular daytrip.

> **Inside Information:** Locals sometimes refer to this fifteenth-century church as 'Addolorata', meaning 'sorrowful' or 'pained'.

Church of Sant'Orsola, Erice. Bepsimage, Istock

Side Trip

Once you see the crystal clear waters of the island of Favignana, you won't believe your luck with how easy it is to get to. The hydrofoil from Trapani takes only twenty-five minutes. You can reach Trapani from Palermo in just over an hour by car though there are coaches available.

The island, the largest of the Egadi Islands, is a well known holiday spot for Italians but seemingly undiscovered by tourists. It is booked solid between June and September; you need to book well in advance if you hope to visit. With so much to see, you may want to consider spending a night or two.

The island is known for a few things. It's popular with scuba divers, from beginners to advanced cave diving. Renting a boat for the day is also very popular and no licence is required. Hiking to the top of a steep hill with the abandoned Santa Caterina Castle is worth it for its incredible view over all of the Egadi Islands. The beaches on the island are rock, with the exception of the sandy Lido Burrone.

The island is closely associated with red tuna fishing, and the former Florio Tuna Factory Museum (Ex Stabilimento Florio delle Tonnare di Favignana e Formica) is popular. It also houses a sea turtle rescue clinic, a marine archaeology exhibit, a room dedicated to the battle of the Egadi Islands and extensive information about tuna processing. You'll never look at a can of tuna the same way again. You'll also find several bronze warship rams, dating from a battle during the First Punic War; a few display scratches from where they made contact. The tours take an hour and can be booked in English.

Other Points of Interest

Palazzo dei Normanni (Norman Palace)
Art and history lovers will enjoy this place. Construction began on the Norman Palace (often called the Royal Palace) in the twelfth century by King Roger II. The palace was home to the kings of Sicily and is currently the seat of the Sicilian Regional Assembly. The dazzling Palatine Chapel (1132) is the star attraction; in 2015 it was included in the UNESCO World Heritage List. Every surface is covered in a glittering mosaic which is original to the period. The palace serves as an outstanding example of Norman-Arabic-Byzantine style.

Catacombe dei Cappuccini (Capuchin Catacombs), Piazza Cappuccini, 1
Some will consider the catacombs, containing more than 1,200 bodies, to be a macabre and bizarre showcase of skeletons. That's an unfortunate assessment and not in line with the original intention of the Capuchin monks.

Why did they do this? In brief, to make you (the visitor) feel alive. The bodies serve as a momento mori, a reminder of death. They encourage the visitor to feel gratitude that they are still alive, to reflect upon how transitory life is and to act. Every skeleton here was once a living person with their own story, just like you. As you see each of them, you'll wonder about their life course, what made them happy, what made them regret things, and what they would have done differently. It will be difficult not to ask yourself the same questions because, as the catacombs remind you, every one of us will inevitably end up as they are: dead. The catacombs therefore are not a morbid curiosity; they are meant to motivate you to live with intention and not postpone important matters.

> 'Remembering that I'll be dead soon is the most important tool I've ever encountered to help me make the big choices in life. Almost everything – all external expectations, all pride, all fear of embarrassment or failure – these things just fall away in the face of death, leaving only what is truly important. Remembering that you are going to die is the best way I know to avoid the trap of thinking you have something to lose. You are already naked. There is no reason not to follow your heart.'
>
> Steve Jobs

The mummies are the result of dehydration, a natural process with limited intervention needed by the living. Kept in an environment with optimal temperature and humidity for six months to a year, the bodies are redressed and placed in a wall niche, open coffin, and sometimes posed in chairs or on benches.

In 1783 it was agreed that anyone who could afford to be mummified and stored in the catacombs could be so. It became a status symbol to have the catacombs as your final resting place, in part because the price was so high that only the wealthy elite could afford it. Families would routinely visit their deceased loved ones. Eventually, the skeletons were divided by gender and occupation; there is even a corridor for virgins and children too.

Chemical embalming was rarely used but there are a few exceptions. The most famous resident of the catacombs is a two-year-old named Rosalia Lombardo, often called 'Sleeping Beauty'. She is so remarkably preserved it looks as if she could wake up at any second. You'll see Rosalia in the chapel, with a yellow ribbon in her hair.

The mummies are also contributing to science. In 2007, the Sicily Mummy Project was created to methodically understand the mummies from an anthropological and palaeopathological standpoint using X-rays, CT Scans and other methods. Researching how they died can lead us to breakthroughs in understanding modern-day disease and epidemics, among other things. I guess you can say that the mummies of Palermo serve to remind us of death but, now, may help us to live longer too.

Always check the website to ensure they are open especially since the catacombs are a bit out of town. There is very little in the way of signage, and visitors are encouraged to draw their own conclusions.

MAINLAND ITALY

> 'You may have the universe if I may have Italy.'
>
> Giuseppe Verdi, Italian Composer, 1813–1901.

While Rome isn't the primary backdrop for the Godfather trilogy, it does play a subtle yet significant role in the films. The Eternal City serves as a canvas upon which the Corleone family's power and influence extend beyond Sicily. In *The Godfather Part III*, Vatican City becomes a pivotal setting, and Michael Corleone's negotiations with the Vatican Bank unfold against the backdrop of St Peter's Basilica. The juxtaposition of organised crime and the sacred enclave adds a layer of complexity to the narrative. Though not the primary filming location, Rome, with its grandeur and historic richness, becomes a symbolic extension of the Corleone saga, where power dynamics transcend geographical boundaries.

Francis Ford Coppola and his crew chose to use several locations in mainland Italy for the second and third films. Two locations in Viterbo were used,

Ancient Rome. Miguel Virkkunen Carvalho, Flikr

which is less than ninety minutes by car from Vatican City. Most recognisable may be the wholesale fish market of Trieste, which served as Ellis Island in New York, and where Young Vito first stepped foot in America as so many other Sicilians did in the early twentieth century.

> **Il Grande Mercato Ittico all'Ingrosso (Wholesale Fish Market), Riva Nazario Sauro, 1, Trieste**
>
> **Scene(s) GF II:**
> - *Young Vito is processed through Ellis Island.*

Background

The Wholesale Fish market in Trieste, Italy served as a stand-in for New York's Ellis Island. Located on the Adriatic Sea and very close to the borders of both Slovenia and Croatia, it's the most remote Godfather filming location in Italy.

The real Ellis Island proved impossible to film at as the historic site had not been renovated when *The Godfather Part II* was being shot between October 1973 and June 1974. Fortunately, the Trieste fish market provided the space and light needed to set the scene.

The nickname for the building is 'Santa Maria del Guato': 'Santa Maria' is a reference to the church-like shape of the building and 'guato' is the local name for a certain kind of fish. It's fully restored and used as an exhibition space, where it can be visited depending on the event schedule.

Scene Analysis: It's 1901, nine-year-old Vito has escaped Corleone for America, arriving at Ellis Island in New York. Immigrants to the United States were processed on the Island prior to entry. People from all over the world, wearing their native dress, are waiting in the Registry Room.

Arguably, one of the most cold and austere scenes across the trilogy, it shows the transition from the warmth of Sicily, through the industrial facility of Ellis Island and, fifty-seven years later, the luxury of Lake Tahoe. Vito, alone in his cell and singing, segues to a party at the family mansion, complete with an entire orchestra. The American dream, arriving with nothing and ending up with an empire of wealth and security, but an inverted one, obtained through criminality and immorality rather than honest work.

Within six decades the Corleones have become American nobility.

How did he go wrong? Vito's first introduction to America is a negative one. The immigration officer, impatient, absently assigns him a new identity. His surname is now, erroneously, the village he was born in. He is marked with an 'x', separated from the others, and quarantined.

Time and again when watching films within the gangster genre the same explanation is given; turning to crime is a product of necessity. Immigrants, denied access to mainstream America, are forced to work outside of their adopted country's laws. Disregard for his identity and, isolated from the other immigrants, the Ellis Island scene is a familiar (and flawed) excuse for why a gangster would import the same patterns of violence that he escaped from.

The fish market in Trieste served as Ellis Island.
Paramount Studios

> 'When plunder becomes a way of life for a group of men in a society, over the course of time they create for themselves a legal system that authorises it and a moral code that glorifies it.'
>
> Frédéric Bastiat

Did You Know?

The film is accurate regarding protocol for immigrants arriving to Ellis Island.

Upon arrival, they would be observed from above to look for signs of weakness, obvious mental illness or difficulty breathing. Once through, the doctor, with the aid of an interpreter, would examine each person. Using chalk, the physician would mark the clothes of immigrants needing further inspection. This happened about 20 percent of the time and these became known as 'the six second physicals'. An 'X' with a circle, as young Vito received, meant the person showed definite signs of disease. Vito showed visible signs of smallpox.

The eye exams were also a reality. Officials were looking for signs of trachoma, which can result in blindness. If an immigrant was judged too sick to work or confirmed to have trachoma, they would be sent back to their home country.

Sick children over the age of twelve would be sent home unaccompanied if deemed too diseased or had pronounced disabilities. Under the age of twelve, one parent would be forced to be sent back home with their child, dividing the family.

Artificial islands, built in the Lower Bay, quarantined those who were sick or had a communicable disease until they were healthy and could be released into the USA. First and second-class passengers that needed quarantine were taken directly off the ship to the quarantine islands while third-class passengers would be required to wait in the registry room for their exam. Not surprisingly, young Vito was a third-class passenger, as we see in the film.

Between 1901 and 1910, one and three quarter million Italians emigrated from Sicily and southern Italy. Many planned to return home. World War I and fascism put a stop to that in the short term. World War II and the resulting economic ruin impeded these ambitions further out. This mass migration would have far-reaching, distressing and often catastrophic consequences, particularly for the rural areas and villages.

Only 2 per cent of immigrants arriving at Ellis Island were denied entry to America.

Chiostro of Santa Maria Della Quercia, Cloister of the Cistern, Viale Fiume, 112, Viterbo, Lazio

Scene(s) GF III:
- *Michael makes a confession to Cardinal Lamberto and admits he killed his brother as well as other sins.*

Background

It is within the cloisters of the Church of Santa Maria Della Quercia that Michael is persuaded to make his confession to Cardinal Lamberto. Michael has just suffered a diabetic attack. He claims that stress causes his blood sugar to drop. The Cardinal asserts that a burdened conscience is the likely cause of bodily suffering and asks Michael if he would like to make a confession. Reluctant at first and claiming he hasn't made one in thirty years, he is persuaded by the Cardinal who assures him that he has nothing to lose.

The grey cloisters of Santa Maria provide a perfect backdrop for a dark confession. The church, which has the status of being a minor basilica, has an interesting history that attracts tourists besides Godfather fans.

In 1417, an artist painted an image of Mary, the Blessed Mother, on a tile and affixed it to an oak tree. This image became a shrine, with miracles attributed to it, specifically during periods of Plague. A chapel was originally built around it, commissioned by the Pope. Eventually, this was enlarged and in 1578 the building we see today was consecrated. 'Quercia'

Cloister of Santa Maria Della Quercia.
Peter1936F, WikiCommons

means oak in Italian, and the basilica is commonly called Madonna of the Oak in reference to the sanctuary. The tile can still be viewed today, enclosed in a marble temple.

There are two cloisters at the basilica. Look for the smaller Cloister of the Cistern to see where Michael's confession took place.

> **Scene Analysis**: This scene is usually remembered because Michael admits out loud to have ordered the death of his brother Fredo. He confesses to other sins, such as betraying his wife. One assumes he is referring to his second wife, Kay, whom, according to Coppola, Michael was married to for six or seven years.
>
> Moreover, he admits to killing men but also to have ordered men to be killed. It's interesting that he specifically makes that distinction.

Did You Know?

Sometimes there is some confusion regarding the sacrament of confession within Catholicism. Confession exists in some form among most religions. Catholics are expected to reconcile their sins by meeting with a priest since priests are the only ones who can grant absolution (forgiveness). The penitent is required to confess mortal sins, which are grave offences, such as murder. They may also confess their venial sins, those of a lesser nature. There is no official list of what constitutes either. However, since Michael queried whether he should make a confession, claiming he doesn't repent, it is surprising to see Cardinal Lamberto absolve him. In reality, a priest cannot offer forgiveness to a person who says they don't feel remorse or regret for their sins.

Palazzo Farnese, Caprarola, Piazza Farnese, Viterbo, Lazio

Scene(s) GF III:
- *Michael meets with Archbishop Gilday to negotiate a $600 million stake in International Immobilare, a property holding company.*
- *Archbishop Gilday chairs a meeting between the owners of Immobilare, Michael Corleone and his legal representative B.J. Harrison (played by George Hamilton).*
- *All interiors of The Vatican, Cardinal Lamberto becomes Pope.*
- *White smoke from the exterior chimney, announcing the appointment of a new Pope.*
- *Archbishop Gilday is murdered by Al Neri on the circular staircase.*

Background

Palazzo Farnese, sometimes called Palazzo Caprarola, sumptuously served as the location for all of the interior scenes set inside the Vatican. Its exterior chimney was also filmed for a brief scene.

The pentagonal-shaped building, which looks like a rectangle from the outside, has a real-life affiliation with the Supreme Pontiff. In 1504, the future Pope Paul III built a rocca on the site, the term used for an Italian fortified stronghold, usually set high on a hilltop and surrounded by the village. In times of trouble, locals could take refuge. These are quite common throughout Italy.

The Pope's grandson took it upon himself to turn the rocca into the Renaissance villa we see today, enlisting the help of one of the greatest architects of his time, Giacomo Vignola. The villa is currently owned by the Accademia Nazionale dei Lincei.

Godfather fans will be interested in two different areas. The scenes with Archbishop Gilday were filmed in the Sala del Mappamondo, otherwise known as the 'room of the world map'. The frescoes were completed in 1574 and display the world as it was known at that time. They were completed by Giovanni Antonio Vanosino de Varese, who also painted at the Vatican. The vault of the room is painted with constellations.

The main spiral staircase where the Archbishop meets his end at the hands of Al Neri is called the Scala Regia. The fresco overhead was painted by Antonio Tempesta. The stairs closely resemble Bramante's Belvedere staircase, which is located at the Vatican itself. In fact, Palazzo Farnese

Palazzo Farnese (Palazzo Caprarola). Jean-Pierre Dalbéra, WikiCommons

Map room of Palazzo Farnese. Jean-Pierre Dalbéra, WikiCommons

is a popular location for filmmakers who need a Vatican stand in as the Vatican itself is notoriously difficult to get permission to film there. Francis Ford Coppola himself has commented that he had difficulties when he was shooting exterior scenes in Rome for *The Godfather Part III*.

In a very brief scene, we see white smoke emanating from the chimney. This represents the ancient practice, still in use, of informing the public that the conclave of Cardinals has voted in a new Pope. This requires a 2/3 majority. If the cardinals cannot come to a consensus, then black smoke would

Scala Regia at Palazzo Farnese. Jean-Pierre Dalbéra, WikiCommons

Fresco by Antonio Tempesta. Jean-Pierre Dalbéra, WikiCommons

spew from the chimney. Eventually, when the papal election is successful, white smoke appears, and a new Pope has been elected. In the case of the film, this was Cardinal Lamberto.

Did You Know?

The Art of the *Aperitivo*

Italians are world famous for living *la dolce vita*, the sweet life. One cultural ritual that exemplifies this: the evening *aperitivo*. Usually between 6pm and 9pm, Italians will enjoy a pre-dinner drink, often alcoholic but not always. The term comes from the Latin word *aperire* which means 'to open' but the true meaning is that it is meant to open your appetite for the evening meal or to stimulate your appetite. Other cultures have a similar practice, sometimes called 'Happy Hour' or just 'pre-dinner cocktails'. I wouldn't suggest comparing *aperitivo* to 'Happy Hour' to an Italian's face though! They consider this ritual to be truly cultural whereas the other is considered a promotional way to sell alcohol at a discounted price. To each their own, but when in Rome...

The origins of the practice are hotly debated. There are claims it started with the ancient Romans, that the Greek doctor Hippocrates introduced it, or that it all began when monks developed herbal elixirs as a medical preparation to treat digestive ailments. The modern day *aperitivo* coincided with the development of vermouth, a fortified wine infused with spices, herbs and other botanicals. There are two distinct versions of it: dry and bitter or otherwise sweet. In the late eighteenth century, Italian apothecary Antonio Benedetto Carpano of Turin is thought to have developed a commercially successful sweet version. He combined muscat with spices and, importantly, sugar and then fortified it with additional alcohol. In the beginning, fashionable urban partakers of the pre-dinner drink would drink vermouth on its own; this is still done today in Italy, France and other European countries, but it isn't common. Where vermouth really gained traction was its use as a cocktail ingredient. The Manhattan gave way to the Martini which spawned the Negroni craze. Either dry or sweet vermouth may be used. If you want equal parts of both, order it as 'perfect' as in a 'perfect Negroni'.

Modern day, as you walk past tables in Italy you'll see bright orange cocktails in large globe wine glasses. Those are usually Aperol or Compari spritzs. It's a mix of prosecco, sparkling water and either of the bitter liqueurs. You may also see the orange Negroni, equal parts Campari, gin and vermouth. Non-drinkers also take part in *aperitivo*, mocktails or soda or whatever your preference. The idea behind the ritual is to relax and socialise. Your drinks will come with a salty snack, usually olives, potato crisps or nuts. If you are looking for a more substantial snack, be on the lookout for *apericena*. *Aperitivo* is a custom you may find yourself repeating when you get home!

Ponte Vittorio Emanuele II, 00186 Rome

Scene(s) GF III:
- *Frederick Keinszig, 'God's Banker', is seen hanging from the bridge; currency falls from his pockets.*
- *Briefly seen just prior to Michael Corleone's arrival by car at the Vatican, St Peter's Basilica is in the background.*

Background

The Ponte Vittorio Emanuele II crosses the Tiber River of Rome with three elegant arches; it was inaugurated in 1911. In this brief scene we see Keinszig hanging from it, St Peter's Basilica in the background. In a previous scene, he was smothered to death with a pillow. As you may recall, Vincent Mancini, newly elevated to the role of a Don, has ordered the deaths of Keinszig, Don Lucchesi and Archbishop Gilday after they attempted to defraud Michael Corleone. Hanging his corpse from a prominent bridge in Rome served as a message.

This plotline has a real life precedent as well. The character of Keinszig is reminiscent of Roberto Calvi, an Italian banker and chairman of Banco Ambrosiano, who was also referred to as 'God's banker'. In 1978, it was discovered that several billion lire (Italian currency) had been illegally exported, resulting in a criminal investigation. Calvi was tried and convicted of fiscal misconduct but was able to keep his position at the bank. In June 1982, two weeks prior to the collapse of the bank, he wrote a letter directly to Pope John Paul II stating that the eminent collapse of the bank would economically injure the Church. On 10 June, the banker fled Italy using a false passport. A little more than a week later he was found hanging from Blackfriars Bridge in London, five bricks in his pockets along with a large amount of money in three different currencies. The Vatican Bank owned substantial shares of Banco Ambrosiano. In 1984, the Vatican Bank agreed to pay $224 million USD as 'recognition of moral involvement'.

The nearby (and more famous) Pont Sant'Angelo has borne witness to a lot of death since it was built. In 1450, it became so overcrowded with religious pilgrims that it partially collapsed,

Ponte Vittorio Emmanuelle II. Lorena Suarez, Flikr

drowning hordes of people. From the 1500s on, for a few centuries, those who were executed in the Piazza di Ponte were subsequently hung from the bridge as a cautionary tale to the general population. Those condemned due to heresy were an especially popular choice.

Vatican City, 00120 Vatican City

Scene(s) GF III:
- Michael Corleone arrives in Rome by car, passing the columns of St Peter's Square.
- St Peter's Basilica is shown as the Pope's death is announced and interspersed variously throughout the film.

Background

Throughout the film we see scenes of St Peter's Square or the dome of the (statue-adorned) rooftop of St Peter's Basilica, usually pictured against the backdrop of a darkening sky. These are located in Vatican City, headquarters of the Roman Catholic church and classified as an independent city-state. There are fewer than a thousand citizens and all serve the church in some capacity. Considering it only has forty-nine hectares, it's the smallest country in the world in terms of size and population.

St Peter's Basilica is at the heart of Vatican City and we see Michael arriving by car outside of its double colonnade

St Peter's Square. David Pirmann, Flikr

and circular piazza. The Basilica itself was built over the tomb of St Peter, an apostle. Coppola, like many film and documentary makers, commented that security at the Square is quite strict and that filming permissions are rarely granted. In order to make his shots, he was told to move his equipment further back.

Atop the façade of the Basilica, seen mostly in silhouette in the film, are thirteen large statues. The middle statue is of Christ the Redeemer. This is flanked by twelve of his apostles, though, curiously, none of them are St Peter himself. A statue of him can be found to the right of the entrance.

In *The Godfather Part III* we get a quick glimpse of the colourfully dressed Swiss Guard. They are a military corps responsible for the personal security of the Pope. All are entitled to Vatican passports and nationality. The Guard was founded in 1506 when the Pope enlisted the help of Swiss mercenaries. Even today, the Vatican maintains a relationship with Switzerland. All potential guard members must be Catholic, at least 174 cm (5'8.5') tall, unmarried, between nineteen and thirty years old and have completed basic training in the Swiss Armed Forces.

The Istituto per le Opere di Religione, also known as the Vatican Bank, is situated in Vatican City and manages the sizable global assets of the Church. If you happen to use an ATM you'll notice they are multilingual. Interestingly, this includes Latin as an option, probably the only ones in the world to do so.

> *'I respectfully submit that everything I put into the movie about the Vatican as a business organization, being venal and mercenary because of its involvement in financial improprieties, is true.'*
> Francis Ford Coppola.

Caravaggio Paintings in Rome

Caravaggio is one of the most famous painters in Italian history. Even those who aren't especially interested in art have heard his name and recognise his dramatic works, his realistic rather than idealised religious paintings, dark and light, the opposite of anything to be seen in Michelangelo's Sistine Chapel. Rome is home to the largest collection of his art, twenty-six pieces in museums, churches and private collections. Fortunately, three churches in Rome house his art and are free to visit.

The Basilica of Santa Maria del Popolo contains two paintings. Look for the Cerasi Chapel (La Capella Cerasi). You'll need to make a small donation to turn the lights on, the paintings are mounted on the side walls. One is *The Conversion of Saint Paul*, the other *The Crucifixion of Saint Peter*. Caravaggio preferred to paint directly onto the canvas without drawing anything first. This makes his paintings even more astonishing. Works by Bernini and Raphael are also located at this minor basilica.

Close to the Piazza Navona lies the Basilica di Sant'Agostino. Here you'll find the *Madonna of Loreto*. The model used to paint Mother Mary was named Lena and was said to be a lover and possibly prostitute with whom Caravaggio was romantically involved. The same model appears most notably in his work *Madonna and Child with St Anne*, or *Madonna and the Serpent*, which can be seen at the Galleria Borghese in Rome. Later, when the model developed a relationship with another man, the jealous Caravaggio attacked him with a sword at a restaurant.

The third church is also near Piazza Navona and the Pantheon, San Luigi dei Francesi, or Church of St Louis of the French. It houses three magnificent works by the painter. Named for Louis IX, King of France, this is the official national church of France in Rome. Towards the front of the church and to the left, look for the Contarelli Chapel. All three paintings have Saint Matthew as their subject matter. Palazzo Madama is just across the street, Corso del Rinascimento. It currently serves as the Senate of the Italian Republic. Caravaggio lived there for four years from 1597.

Francis Ford Coppola commented that he wished he had been able to shoot more of *The Godfather Part III* in New York but due to budget constraints he wasn't able to. While a few streets in New York City were filmed, the majority of the film was shot in Sicily or on a soundstage at Cinecittà Studios in Rome. This includes the party given at Michael Corleone's New York City apartment, the mafia meeting at Atlantic City famously ambushed by a helicopter and the interior scenes for the opera *Cavalleria rusticana*.

Film Facts: *The Godfather Part III* takes place in 1979, twenty years after the ending of the second film. Production for the film started in Rome on 27 November 1989 and finished in New York City. Filming was completed by May of 1990 and *The Godfather Part III* opened in theatres on Christmas Day, 1990.

Life imitates art: How do actual mafia members feel about The Godfather films?

'Shame'.

That was the headline of a usually sedate Italian financial journal after the 20 August 2015 funeral of Vittorio Casamonica in Rome. Casamonica, boss of the notorious mafia clan bearing his name, had a grand send-off. A black and gold gilded carriage drawn by six black horses, plumed, carried his body in a processional to the church in the south-east suburbs from which he operated. Lorries drove through the street, throwing roses. A helicopter flew low overhead, tossing rose petals. It was estimated the funeral drew over 500 mourners. None of this was impeded by the authorities, who claimed they did not know what was about to take place. The parish priest who conducted the funeral service, in a later interview, would also claim the same. The news replayed the spectacle all day and evening much to the outrage of Romans and visitors alike. I know that because I happened to be a visitor to Rome on that same day.

The day before, a judge had set a trial date for fifty-nine people after a mafia investigation revealed increasingly close ties between city government officials and local mob bosses regarding lucrative public contracts. This display of mafia power and influence still proceeded.

There is more to the story. To no one's surprise in Italy but to seemingly everyone's surprise internationally, an orchestra played the theme music from *The Godfather* the entire time.

The films have long been criticised for glamourising the mafia's criminality. In reality, it was the mafia that adopted social cues from the film to authorise their criminal lifestyle, to become men of honour. According to Selwyn Raab, an expert in the field, he bluntly states 'The film validated their lifestyles and decisions to join the Mob and accept its credo.' That does seem to be the case. Wiretaps of mob members and their associates have picked up on several references to the films, all of them positive. In 2005, two New York mafioso were discussing a third person, under investigation. He was referred to as a Luca Brasi type of man. He went on to explain that Luca Brasi was a hitman for the Corleone family. This information proved useful to investigators. Sammy 'The Bull' Gravano, underboss to John Gotti and who has admitted to participating in nineteen murders, claims the films inspired him and cemented his involvement in the mafia. He later said he would look to the films for guidance when making decisions, how to speak and how to act. The same effect was felt in Sicily. After the premiere of the film, one person commented that Marlon Brando was likely the envy of all of the real godfathers on the island. Quite possibly, Vittorio Casamonica and his clan felt that the films also legitimised their business activities.

Did Frankie 'Five Angels' Pentangeli Know his Roman History?

In a remarkable sequence, Tom Hagen pays a visit to Frank Pentangeli, who had collaborated with the FBI to implicate Michael Corleone in court. Witnessing his brother flown in from Sicily during the trial, Pentangeli recants his testimony, claiming ignorance. In a subtle conversation, Tom hints to Pentangeli that taking his own life might be the best course of action. Pentangeli agrees, pointing to a precedent in the Roman Empire where families of conspirators received clemency if the conspirator committed suicide. He then turns to Tom, and affirms that the Corleone Family operates akin to the Roman empire, a sentiment with which Tom concurs.

There are numerous examples in ancient Rome of a similar circumstance.

One example involving clemency for the families of conspirators after suicide can be found in the context of the Year of the Four Emperors (69 CE). During this tumultuous year, after the death of Emperor Nero, multiple claimants vied for control of the Roman Empire, leading to a series of conflicts and power struggles. One of the claimants, Otho, who briefly ruled as emperor, faced a challenge from Vitellius. Otho's forces were defeated and he chose to commit suicide in 69 CE.

Following Otho's death, Vitellius, who became the new emperor, is reported to have shown clemency toward Otho's relatives. According to historical

Tom Hagen visits Frank Pentangeli. Paramount Studios

accounts, Vitellius spared their lives and allowed them to retain their properties. This demonstrates a measure of leniency towards the families of the defeated conspirator. This example illustrates how, in times of political transition or reconciliation, some Roman leaders chose not to pursue harsh consequences for the families of those who had taken their own lives in the aftermath of a failed conspiracy.

On the surface it seems that Frank's Sicilian brother serves as a visual reminder that Pentangeli needs to uphold his silence and honour. There is also a possibility that Frank's brother might have faced harm if Pentangeli were to proceed with his testimony, although this is not explicitly stated.

Other Points of Interest

St Peter's Basilica, Vatican City

It's possible to visit St Peter's Basilica, as seen in the film. The second basilica on the site, it was consecrated in 1626. Catholic tradition holds that it was built over the burial site of the apostle, Saint Peter, his tomb being directly below the high altar. The dome, an iconic and dominating part of the Roman skyline, is the tallest in the world. Visitors are able to climb to the top if they choose; it's over 500 steps. It also serves as the

Rome from St Peter's Dome. Bradley Weber, Flikr

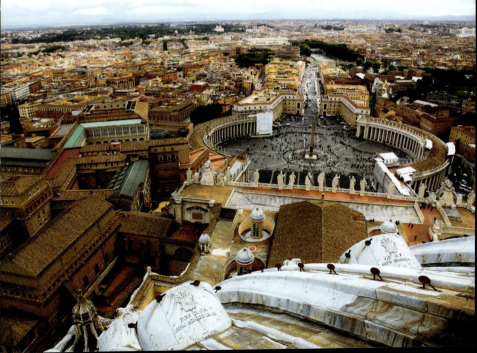

inspiration for other domes, including St Paul's Cathedral in London and the Capital Building in Washington, DC. St Peter's was the largest church in the world until 1989 when an even larger basilica was built in Yamoussoukro, Ivory Coast, Africa.

The Basilica itself is an architectural masterpiece and contains several notable works of art. Bernini, Michelangelo, Raphael and Bramante are all represented. Some of the most popular are Michelangelo's *La Pietà* and the ancient (1300 CE) bronze statue of St Peter sitting on a throne. Visitors will notice that its right foot has been worn thin. Pilgrims since the Middle Ages have touched or kissed the foot, asking him to help them get to heaven if they should die during the pilgrimage.

Some might not be aware that the finances regarding the construction of St Peter's are one of the factors igniting the Reformation and the birth of Protestantism. The commercialisation of indulgences, essentially a reduction in punishment for sins once the applicant is deceased in exchange for a financial contribution, was stated as one reason Martin Luther wrote *The 95 Theses*.

The Basilica is free to enter.

Scala Elicoidale Momo, the Bramante Staircase, Vatican Museums, Vatican City
Palazzo Farnese, Caprarola, Viterbo served as The Vatican for all of the interior scenes in *The Godfather Part III*, including the circular stairs where

Original Bramante Staircase, 1505. daryl_mitchell, WikiCommons

Modern Bramante Staircase, 1932. Victor R. Ruiz, WikiCommons

Archbishop Gilday was killed by Caporegime Al Neri. Those stairs are modelled after the Bramante Staircase, which is actually the name given to two sets of stairs, the original built in 1505 and the modern in 1932. Both are double helix in design; one staircase would have been for going up and the other for descending. Alternatively, separate stairs may have served to divide humans from animals. Neither feature the ornate frescoes of Palazzo Farnese, Caprarola.

Highlights of the original staircase are its Doric columns and herringbone pavers. It looks less like a staircase and more like a ramp, which made it possible for animal use. This is only viewable by appointment.

The modern equivalent was designed by Giuseppe Momo. The balustrade is made of hammered metal and the steps are also shallow and more like a ramp. This staircase, more similar to the one seen in *The Godfather Part II*, is located at the Vatican Museum. In fact, it is the exit for the Pio Clementino Museum.

An interesting aside, the first example ever found of a spiral staircase is back in Sicily! Greek Temple A at Selinunte, built sometime between 490–460 BCE, is the earliest known spiral staircase found to date.

9
CORLEONE, SICILY

> 'They call the Mafia La Piovra, "the octopus," because its tentacles reach into every aspect of daily life, and when one arm is cut off, another grows in its place. Some things haven't changed in centuries.'
>
> Theresa Maggio, *The Stone Boudoir: Travels through the Hidden Villages of Sicily.*

As previously mentioned, Corleone, Sicily, was never filmed for any of the Godfather movies. When the director and his crew were scouting locations, they visited the town but found it to be too urbanised to fulfil the script requirements of Michael's exile: post-war Sicily in the 1940s. They did not receive a warm greeting upon their arrival either. This may have been a factor in declining to work there, having already dealt with similar headaches when filming in New York City. Nevertheless, after the pictures debuted, Corleone became a town recognisable to nearly everyone who hears the name. Though immortalised in Puzo's book and Coppola's masterpiece films, it was a notable and unfortunately accurate entry to the mafia lexicon long before the 1970s. Corleone is located in the dry interior of the island, in the valley of a mountainous area. It's only an hour from Palermo by car. Having a good understanding of the roads you need to take is advised as the signs reading 'Corleone' are repeatedly stolen. Whether this is the work of overzealous Godfather fans is yet to be determined. The arid, rocky landscapes depicted, especially in the first two films, are representative of the town's environment and geology. The dry river bed where Antonio Andolini's funeral procession takes place during the opening scene of *The Godfather Part II* could easily be mistaken for the flat mountain Rocca Busambra, the highest nearby peak. Fiction coincides with reality as its parent range, the Monti Sicani, has functioned as an illicit burial site and dumping ground for those who either mustered the courage to challenge mafia domination or, at the other end of the spectrum, chose to become an active member but became disposable when no longer needed or wanted.

Corleone, Sicily. TisPhotovision, iStock

That Corleone has been in the grips of one of the mafia's most violent and brutal clans would be an understatement. Its history may have inspired Mario Puzo's use of it in *The Godfather* book. For over half a century the town's people were subjugated and silenced by the Corleonesi clan, who ran the town like their own personal kingdom. The mafia system itself was no sudden occurrence. The feudal system in Sicily existed for over 800 years, with landowners using their private armies to both manage their estates and enforce the collection of rents from the peasants. Officially this ended in 1812 though in reality, the system didn't end overnight. Some would say evidence exists for patron/client systems dating back to ancient Rome. This, combined with Sicily's long history of foreign invasion and occupation, makes it no stranger to power imbalances between the people and their governors. Mafia bosses replaced former Sicilian land barons in a succession that has been played out in Sicily for centuries.

Concurrent with the films, the 1970s saw the rise of Salvatore 'Totò' Riina (also called 'The Beast'), Bernardo Provenzano, Luciano Leggio and other affiliates all hailing from Corleone. No Sicilian alive during the 1980s has forgotten The Second Mafia War, often called the 'Mattanza' (Italian for 'Slaughter') that saw homicides not in the hundreds but in the thousands. That figure includes bystanders, all considered collateral damage. The instigators were the Corleonesi and their rivals, the established bosses of several Palermo mafia clans. Sheer brute force was their strategy.

Even young children aren't spared this memory as the conflict left many without one or both parents. Children themselves were victims, including Salvatore 'Totuccio' Inzerillo's fifteen-year-old son. Inzerillo, leader of Palermo's Passo di Rigano family, was taken down in public by a team of hitmen wielding rifles in May of 1981. Witnesses remained passive, obeying the rule of omertà. His young son, swearing revenge at his father's funeral, was kidnapped and tortured to death with a machete a month later. His arm was dismembered before his death, symbolic of the arm that would have been used to shoot Salvatore 'Totò' Riina in retaliation.

The victim's father was a prolific heroin trafficker with substantial ties to the United States mob. This included his relative, New York City mafia boss Carlo Gambino. No longer just a waystation for drugs produced in Turkey, Lebanon, Afghanistan and other countries (as established by the 1957 Palermo Mafia Summit), Sicilians founded their own laboratories, supplanting the French Connection altogether. By the time of Inzerillo's death, it was believed that 65–70 percent of heroin originated on the island. Italy's High Commissioner estimated that the Sicilian mafia numbered between 5,000 to 10,000 adherents in the 1980s, most backed up with brothers, nephews, cousins and others, making that number exponentially larger. The population of Sicily at that time was fewer than five million. This drugs bonanza fueled the power struggle and intensified the rivalry. Initially, the Palermitani referred to Corleonisi as 'the peasants' ('viddani' in Sicilian) with regard to their hinterland origins. Later they would realise their mistaken underestimation, the few left alive to do so when the war was over at the end of 1982, that is. The Corleonisi clan were the clear victors, with fewer casualties. The Italians sometimes call the dark days of the '70s and '80s the 'years of lead'. However, the violence dragged on into the '90s. The remaining rivals allied themselves with the Corleonisi but Riina's paranoia and megalomania did not assure safety for anyone. Friend or foe, everyone was disposable, their families included. Riina 'The Beast' didn't share Michael Corleone's philosophy that only his enemies needed to be wiped out.

So emboldened would this clan from rural Corleone become that between

1992 and 1993, they waged war against the Italian State itself. A campaign of violence left police chiefs, politicians and even a general of the Carabinieri murdered. These victims were referred to as '*cadaveri eccellenti*', excellent cadavers, in Italy due to their public high profiles. A duo of anti-mafia prosecutors, Giovanni Falcone and Paolo Borsellino, worked to combat the tidal wave of violence. This resulted in the Maxi Trial of 1986, where hundreds of Mafiosi were convicted of a laundry list of crimes. The trial took place in a purpose-built bunker-style courtroom located inside the walls of the prison holding the accused. Salvatore 'Totò' Riina, a fugitive, was given two life sentences *in absentia*. Both prosecutors along with family members and police escorts were later murdered on his orders in 1992.

In both Palermo and Corleone as well as other parts of Sicily, you can see memorials built to honour their martyrdoms. In Corleone today, on the side of a school wall, one can see the giant mural of Francesca Morvillo, Giovanni Falcone's wife, who was killed alongside her husband in a car bombing. The main square itself is dedicated to Falcone and Borsellino.

Falcone & Borsellino tribute, one of many in Sicily. Casey Hugelfink, iStock

Riina, a fugitive for 23 years, was arrested in January 1993 and died in custody in 2017.

Unfortunately, this isn't the end of the story; real life doesn't resemble the movies with a repentant Michael Corleone figure. As recently as December of 2023, the prosecutor of Palermo, Maurizio de Lucia, commented on the mafia's ability to socially adapt. As a result of a campaign of convicting mafiosi over the last few decades, women's roles in the organisational structure have substantially evolved out of necessity. The last twenty years have seen a profound integration of women in operational roles not seen in the past.

Historically, women had a secondary role, acting as messengers between imprisoned members and the outside world. Their services as couriers came with the assumption that the police neglected to observe women. They also assumed that females lacked the cunning needed for criminal enterprise. This has changed. While the Sicilian mafia still maintains its patriarchy, women are increasingly being trained to take command when their fathers and brothers are jailed or dead. The latest investigations are making clear that women are giving orders, sometimes without needing their imprisoned relative's consent. Subordinates are accepting them. These Godmothers are proving strategic in the survival of the modern-day Cosa Nostra while increasing the boundaries of Sicily's police and judiciary.

So where does this leave Corleone today? Still fatigued by mafia war and adhering to omertà or actively trying to rebrand themselves away from the stereotypes? It's a mix of both. In April of 2023, Giuseppe Salvatore Riina, the third-born child of Totò, returned home to Corleone after serving eight years in prison for money laundering, extortion and mob association. The local government, headed by the anti-mafia mayor Nicolò Nicolosi, voted for a resolution demanding his 'swift removal' from the town, citing him as an unwelcome citizen and noting the damage that his family had inflicted upon the reputation of the town. The decision came about after observing the townspeople being polite to him upon his return, less out of respect and more out of fear, according to the mayor. There are residents of Corleone who disagree with the resolution, a surprising mix of older residents living in the past and younger citizens attracted to the supposed glamour of the Cosa Nostra lifestyle. As for Riina Jr, he claims he is being harassed and persecuted.

Surprisingly (or maybe not), locals report the arrival of tourists who mistakenly believe that the movies were filmed in town. Liborio Grizzafi, manager of the anti-mafia project Intus, reported telling a tourist that the sixteenth-century church he was posing in front of wasn't used in the film at all. The deflated tourist responded that he had travelled from Colombia just to see it. Regardless, if a visitor to Sicily decides to make the trek to Corleone, they will find a few attractions hoping to capitalise on a Godfather pilgrimage. A couple of cafés, getting into the spirit of things, are adorned with movie posters and photos. Perhaps a bit confusing, but a museum exists in the centre of town called 'The Godfather's House'. It's a mansion dating to the 1800s and not associated with the film. While it has great reviews, a few tourists have written online critiques expressing confusion and disappointment. Remember, only the exterior of Don Vito's birthplace was ever filmed and that filming location is in Forza d'Agrò, on the East Coast.

An hour in the car from Palermo is well worth the time to visit Corleone's outstanding anti-mafia museum dedicated to telling the real stories. Quite the mouthful, the Centro Internazionale di Documentazione sulla Mafia e del Movimento Antimafia is generally called the CIDMA Museum. This moving museum was inaugurated in 2000 with high-ranking politicians and diplomats in attendance, including Pino Arlacchi, the Deputy Secretary-General of the United Nations. Brave locals serve as enthusiastic English-speaking guides. The museum is divided into several rooms. The first room contains copies of the Maxi Trial documents. The mountain of files extends from floor to ceiling. The sheer volume of the documentation is impressive and a tribute to the work and commitment of Giovanni Falcone and Paolo Borsellino.

The 'Room of Messages' is both shocking and heartbreaking. It houses the photos of the well-known Sicilian photographer Letizia Battaglia who worked as a photojournalist for the now defunct newspaper L'Ora. She was courageous enough to photograph mafia murder scenes in explicit detail during the 1970s and 1980s. The result is a visual testimony against the mafia and their barbaric tactics, a direct response to the romanticised Hollywood portrayals of the mafia. Shown are photos of men, women and children, their bodies sometimes posed and played with after their death; the mafia was sending a clear message.

The 'Room of Pain' exhibits the photos of Shobha, Letizia Battaglia's daughter, who followed in her mother's footsteps. The abject despair of family members brought to the murder scene to identify their relatives is not easily forgotten. The philosophy behind the museum: the consequences of mafia crime must be transparent, no matter how raw.

Finally, the Carlo Alberto Dalla Chiesa room is dedicated to General Dalla Chiesa, who was assassinated along with his wife and police escort in 1982 during the 'years of lead'. His death led to the approval of a sweeping set of anti-mafia laws that the General had unsuccessfully pleaded for prior to his murder. These included the ability to examine bank records to trace asset transfers, increased use of wiretaps against suspected mafiosi and, interestingly, the ability to interrogate witnesses behind closed doors, in an effort to break the Sicilian code of silence, omertà. This room has photos of mafia bosses set directly next to the people in the legal system who fought against them.

Since 1996, the Italian government has distributed land and other assets confiscated by the mafia and returned them to farmers and other citizens to put to honest use. Residents of Corleone are some of the recipients of these large land holdings. The program had a rough start. Many residents were afraid to set up cooperatives, fearing they would be killed. They were not unjustified in this thinking. Crops planted in the first year were cut down or set alight and other businesses set up were vandalised and the new owners threatened. The Placido Rizzotto cooperative was assigned 200 hectares of land in 2002, previously owned by Totò Riina. It was used to produce what they label 'anti-mafia pasta' and other products under the Libera Terra brand. They were unable to find a company to provide a harvester during their first year; not one harvester in the Corleone countryside was willing to take the risk. The police intervened. Placido Rizzotto carried on and today the cooperative gives employment to vulnerable individuals who otherwise may be attracted to organised crime. Thanks to anti-mafia support, they are now financially self-sufficient and considered a pioneer and model for other cooperatives set up on confiscated lands. Though they still suffer fires, harassment and boycotts throughout the two decades they have been in business, they persevere.

The Museum of Legality ('Laboratorio della Legalita') on Cortile Colletti 3 Traversa Di Via Coletti is located in one of the confiscated houses. The property was formally owned by the ruthless Bernardo Provenzano, known as 'Bernie the Tractor' for mowing down anyone who happened to get in his way. He was second in command to Salvatore Riina, taking command in the outside world when Riina was arrested. Like Riina, he received life sentences *in absentia* during the Maxi Trial in the late 80s and was also involved and convicted in the Falcone and Borsellino bombings. A native of Corleone, his life of criminality started very early in his adolescence. In 1963 he became a fugitive after a failed hit on the supporter of an already deceased rival. The family of the man issued a vendetta on his life. In addition, the police issued a warrant for his arrest. He would remain a fugitive for forty-three years. It was in 1981, while on the run, that Provenzano

Addiopizzo Travel tour of Corleone. Addiopizzo Travel

and Riina put into motion the bloody Second Mafia War, killing many of the established Palermo heads of families to gain control over the lucrative heroin trade.

He managed to evade the law for more than four decades due to a combination of paranoia and collaboration with helpful local political authorities. The only known photo of him was from 1959. Refusing to use telephones, he issued orders using small, handwritten notes. So entrenched is the mafia that a word exists in Italian specifically to refer to small notes used for communication by mafiosi: 'pizzini'. Provenzano's pizzini are easy to assign to him. Not only did he encrypt his messages using Caesar cipher (replacing letters with numbers) but his increasing religious fervor meant he included blessings alongside assassination instructions. He was known to dress in bishop's clothing. Provenzano was eventually captured living in a farmhouse outside of Corleone in 2006, dying in prison ten years later.

The Museum of Legality makes great use of confiscated property once belonging to Bernie The Tractor. It contains 53 paintings by the Sicilian painter Gaetano Porcasi portraying the history and mafia brutality over the last several decades. It also tells the story of Bernardo Provenzano.

Corleone is keen to rehabilitate its image, with a mayor at the helm who has no issue in stating so. The mafia will never be completely stamped out. Even General Dalla Chiesa, just before his death, remarked that his goal wasn't to beat the mafia but rather to try to contain it. Addiopizzo Travel operates a popular tour in Corleone, focusing on the anti-mafia resistance movement and telling stories that most people have never heard. Entry to the Museum of Legality is included. They also focus on something that is often overlooked: the uniquely beautiful environment of Corleone and its rural surroundings.

ACKNOWLEDGEMENTS

Endless thanks to the wonderful professionals at White Owl and Pen & Sword Books Limited: Jonathan Wright, Charlotte Mitchell, Kate Bohdanowicz, Paul Wilkinson and Janet Brookes. I couldn't have wished for a more supportive team as a new author.

Mille grazie to Mario Triolo. When I reached out to him and requested permission to use one of his photos that I came across online, he generously shared 150 images of his picturesque hometown, Forza d'Agrò. His enthusiasm for promoting it is truly commendable.

My gratitude to Andrea Morabita of Savoca who provided numerous photos of both his charming restaurant, Dioniso, and the village itself. Savoca is lucky to have a restaurant that matches its own magic. I can't wait to return.

Thanks to the women of Le Mamme del Borgo, who supplied me with photos of the culinary experience they have created for visitors to Motta Camastra. I'm looking forward to trying the arancini with wild fennel! I'm pleased to finally set the record straight that Motta Camastra was the first glimpse of 'Corleone' we see in *The Godfather*.

My greatest appreciation to the grassroots movement Addiopizzo who works to rid Sicily of mafia extortion and to the business owners brave enough to become members. Words fall short of conveying my admiration. Thank you for the photos.

Thanks to Nigel J. Hetherington, CEO of Past Preservers, who suggested I submit a writing sample to a publisher. Thanks also to Theresa Maggio for allowing me to use a quote from her book and Villa La Limonaia for the photos. Many thanks to my mother Mary, who encouraged me to write, my sister Kerry, who offered her input, and my brother-in-law Ralph who couldn't have been happier for me. Thanks to my dear friend Sammie who somehow predicted this would all happen.

To the Mexicans I live among who unknowingly inspire me daily with their attitudes toward life, *muchas gracias*.

And for Dr Paul Spence, my husband of 22 years, who chauffeurs me to the most remote corners of Italy without a word of complaint.

BIBLIOGRAPHY

'Corleone: da domani al via il convegno 'Via la mafia dalla Sicilia' con esperti e forze ordine'. *La Sicilia*, 30 November 2023.

'Family Reunion'. *People*, 24 March 1997.

'I Gambino di New York, il clan Che ha Ispirato la Saga de 'Il Padrino'. *La Sicilia*, 8 November 2023.

'Mafia Insisted on Its Own Preview of 'Godfather,' Producer Reveals.' *Box Office*, 17 December 1973.

'Puzo, Ruddy Deny Friction on 'Godfather.'' *Hollywood Reporter*, 11 March 1971.

'*Shooting The Mob*'. Directed by Kim Longinotto. Modern Films, 2019.

'Show Business: the final act of a family epic'. *TIME*, 16 December 1974.

'Taormina Film Festival Begins Today'. (26 June 2022). Retrieved from www.vitagazette.com/en/68-taormina-film-festival-starts-today

'*The Godfather and the Mob*'. Directed by Simon George. Class Films, 2006.

'*The Godfather: DVD Collection*'. Paramount Pictures, 2001.

'*The Godfather: The Coppola Restoration Bonus Materials*'. Directed by Francis Ford Coppola. Paramount Pictures, 2008.

'The Making of 'The Godfather.'' *Time*, 13 March 1972.

'The Sicily You Like: Savoca, Knowledge and Flavors.' *Gazzetta Ionica*. 6 August 2023.

Abrams, Norma, and Stephen Brown. 'Mafia Chief Organizes a Picket Line at the FBI.' *New York Daily News*, 1 May 1970.

Addiopizzo Travel. (n.d.). www.addiopizzotravel.it

Addiopizzo.org. (n.d.). www.addiopizzo.org

Admin. (29 January 2023). 'Exploring the Beauty and History of Taormina-Giardini Train Station in Sicily'. Sicily Lab. www.sicilylab.com

Adminanswers. (23 May 2013). What is the difference between mortal and venial sin? Catholic Straight Answers. (n.d.) www.catholicstraightanswers.com/what-is-the-difference-between-mortal-and-venial-sin/

Allen, Alesha. 'The complex meaning of the word 'Auguri''. *Italy Magazine*, 19 April 2014.

Amenta, M., Ballistreri, G., Fabroni, S., Romeo, F. V., Spina, A., & Rapisarda, P. (2015). Qualitative and nutraceutical aspects of lemon fruits grown on the mountainsides of the Mount Etna: A first step for a protected designation of origin or protected geographical indication application of the brand name 'Limone dell'Etna.' *Food Research International*, 74, 250–259.

American Film Institute Catalog. (n.d.). www.catalog.afi.com/

AP. 'Cosa Nostra Men Cleared In Sicily; 7 from U.S. are among 17 acquitted in rackets case'. *The New York Times*, 26 June 1968.

AP. 'Italy seizes 10 in the mafia linked with gang in U.S.; Raids Abroad Net Leaders Of Mafia'. *The New York Times*, 3 August 1965.

AP. 'Vatican Payment Reported'. *The New York Times*, 26 May 1984.

Arena, Jenny. (5 July 2022). 'Confetti: Symbolic sugared almonds. Buonissimo'. www.buonissimo.ca/

Balletta, L., & Lavezzi, A. M. (December 2023). 'The economics of extortion: Theory and the case of the Sicilian Mafia'. *Journal of Comparative Economics*, 51(4), 1109–1141.

Bar Vitelli. (n.d.). 'The Godfather.' www.barvitelli.it/

Barbagallo, & Calvi, F. 'Geomechanical study and rock fall hazard analysis in the historical Centre of Forza d'Agrò (Messina - Italy)'. *IOP Conference Series: Earth and Environmental Science*, 833(1), 012174, 2021.

Bastiat, F. *Economic sophisms, 2nd series, Chapter 1* [J. Willems and M. Willems, Trans.]. Carmel: *Liberty Fund*. (Original work pub. 1848).

Bazilian, E. (17 November 2022). "The White Lotus' heads to Sicily for a second season of elegance and mayhem'. *Frederic Magazine*. www.fredericmagazine.com

BBC On This Day 1982 June 19. ' 'God's banker' found hanged'. *BBC*, 19 June 1982.

Benato, M. et al.' 'We came away awestruck': 13 writers on Europe's hidden treasures, from Chagall in Kent to Rome's secret Caravaggios'. *The Guardian*, 13 January 2024.

Benítez Hernández, P., Valiente López, M. (2015) 'The Tangent Solution to the Late Gothic Helical Staircase: A Justified Oblivion'. *Nexus Netw J* 17, 379–398.

Cattedrale Acireale: SS Annunziata. (n.d.). www.beweb.chiesacattolica.it/

Biographical Dictionary of Italians. (2002). Gregorietti, Salvatore. www.treccani.it/

Blok, Anton, *The mafia of a Sicilian Village, 1860-1960*. New York: Harper & Row, 1968.

Boffey, D. 'Scientists hope to unravel mystery of Sicily's child mummies'. *The Guardian*, 5 January 2022.

Bohlen, C. 'Palermo Journal; After the Mafia, a sort of children's crusade'. *The New York Times*, 10 March 1995.

Brancato, Annamaria. 'The counterclockwise clock of the Cathedral of Savoca'. *Armando Siciliano Editore*. 2016.

Brydone, Patrick, Beckford, William. A tour through Sicily and Malta. In a series of letters to William Beckford, Esq. of Somerly in Suffolk; from P. Brydone, F.R.S. ; In two volumes. Boston: Printed by Joseph Bumstead, for John Boyle, David West, and E. Larkin, Jun. 1792.

Burr, Ty. 'How "Godfather" DVDs reveal a director's ego'. *Entertainment Weekly*, 25 October 2001.

C.I.D.M.A. (n.d.). www.cidmacorleone.it

Caffè Bar San Giorgio. (n.d.). www.barsangiorgio.com/

Calandra, Enrico. *Breve storia dell'architettura in Sicilia*. Venice: Testo & Immagine, 1996.

Cameron, Sue. "Godfather' Biggest Thing Since GWTW, Al Ruddy Says.' *Hollywood Reporter*, 6 November 1970.

Camilleri, Andrea. '*You Don't Know: A Mafia Dictionary*.' Translated by Elizabeth Harris. Words Without Borders, 30 November 2012.

Canby, Vincent. 'A Moving and Brutal 'Godfather." *New York Times*, 16 March 1972.

Cantor, Paul. 'I Believe in America: The Godfather Story and the Immigrant's Tragedy' In *Pop Culture and the Dark Side of the American Dream: Con Men, Gangsters, Drug Lords, and Zombies*. Lexington: University Press of Kentucky, 17 May 2019.

Castelmola almond wine (n.d.). www.enjoysicilia.it

Castelmola. (2024). L'Associazione de I Borghi Più Belli D'Italia. www.borghipiubelliditalia.it

Catacombe Frati Cappuccini (n.d.). www.catacombefraticappuccini.com

Catanzaro, Raimondo, *Men of Respect: A Social History of the Sicilian Mafia*. New York: The Free Press, Macmillan, 1992.

Cavalleria Rusticana/Pagliacci. (n.d.). www.metopera.org

Chaney, Edward. *The Evolution of the Grand Tour*. London and New York: Routledge, 1998.

Chellsen, Alex. 'Never Let Your Body Show What You're Thinking: Gesture and Masculinity in The Godfather'. *The Godfather Anatomy of a Film*, 2018.

Cliff, Andrew D. et al., 'Controlling The Geographical Spread Of Infectious Disease: Plague In Italy, 1347–1851'. *Acta med-hist Adriat* 2009;7(1);197236.

Coder, K. D. (12 October 2021). 'Your black walnut tree is out to get you'. www.newswire.caes.uga.edu

Commune di Motta Camastra. (2024). Regione Siciliana. www.comunemottacamastra.it

Commune di Savoca. (2024). Regione Siciliana. www.comune.savoca.me.it/hh/index.php

Comune di Trieste. (n.d.). www.comune.trieste.it/

Coppola, Francis Ford. *The Godfather Notebook*. New York: Regan Arts, 2016.

D'Emilio, Frances. 'Bernardo Provenzano, Sicilian Mafia 'boss of bosses,' dies at 83.' *The Washington Post*, 14 July 2016.

D'Ignoti, Stefania. (25 February 2022). The gender fight behind Sicily's most iconic snack. BBC Travel.

Dewey, Caitlin. 'How the 19th Century Lemon Craze gave rise to the infamous Sicilian mob.' *The Washington Post*, 19 January 2018.

Di Borgo, A. P. (29 October 2022). 'Why is the Sicilian lemon (Siracusa, PGI) so popular?' www.orizzonte-magazine.com

Diego Gambetta, *The Sicilian Mafia: The Business Of Private Protection*. Cambridge, MA: Harvard University Press, 1993.

Dio, Cassius. *Roman History, Volume VIII: Book 64*. Translated by Earnest Cary, Herbert B. Foster. Loeb Classical Library 37. Cambridge: Harvard University Press, 1914.

Distefano, L. 'Donne e mafia, De Lucia: Cresciute per essere addestrate a diventare boss'. *La Sicilia*, 17 December 2023.

Driscoll, Molly. "The Godfather': 10 behind-the-scenes stories about the making of the Classic Films'. *The Christian Science Monitor*, 2 February 2012.

Dunham, S. (11 August 2023). 'Everyone's a Tony – The Story of St Anthony Abbot'. www.lifeinabruzzo.com

'E' Morto Corrado Gaipa'. Archivio La Repubblica.it, 23 September 1989.

Ellis Island - Medical examination. (n.d.). www.ellisisland.se

Emanuele. 'Il Padrino-50 anni e non sentirli'. *Il Giornale di Forza d'Agrò*, 10 February 2022.

Emanuele. 'Un'altra Corleone in Sicilia Qui Coppola inventò Il Padrino'. *Il Giornale di Forza d'Agrò*, 7 February 2021.

Evans, Robert. *The Kid Stays in the Picture: A Notorious Life*. New York: It Books, 2013.

Facebook. (n.d.). www.facebook.com/acirealesocial/posts/castello-scammacca-dei-pennisi-di-floristella-in-vendita-in-vendita-per-5-milion/1747001105438532/

Falcone, Giovanni. *Men of Honour: The Truth about the Mafia*. London: Fourth Estate, 1991. Fentress, James. *Rebels and Mafiosi: Death in a Sicilian Landscape*. New York: Cornell University Press, 2000.

Ferretti, Fred. 'Italian-American League's Power Spreads'. *New York Times*, 4 April 1971.

Filippo, M.S. (1 October 2019). 'Properly reading an Italian menu'. www.thoughtco.com/

Fiumefreddo Di Sicilia Encyclopedia, *Science News & Research Reviews*. (n.d.). Academic Accelerator. www.academic-accelerator.com

Fondazione Giuseppe Whitaker. (n.d.). www.villamalfitano.it/

Fondazione Teatro Massimo. (16 January 2024). Teatro Massimo. www.teatromassimo.it/

Forza d'Agrò, Images of the Nativity in the Church of St. Francis. *Gazzetta Ionica*. 29 December 2011.

Forza D'Agrò. (2008). Commune Forza D'agrò. www.forzadagro.net

Forza D'Agro e la storia. (n.d.). 'Cenni storici'. www.forzadagro.org

Fratelli Branca Distillerie. (18 July 2017). *The history Carpano*. www.carpano.com

Funivia Etna. (17 November 2023). Escursioni Funivia Etna. www.funiviaetna.com

Garrett, S. 'Francis Ford Coppola: What I've learned'. *Esquire*, 29 June 2022.

Gatto, Cristina. (10 May 2018). 'Borgo di Savoca: a town with seven faces and a fertile land of strong talents'. www.en.italiani.it

Gelmis, Joseph. 'Merciful Heavens, Is This The End of Don Corleone?' *New York Magazine*, 23 August 1971.

Giorgie. (7 March 2023). Turrisi Bar in Sicily: the famous café with phalluses inside. *Quiiky Magazine*.

Glatter K.A., Finkelman P. 'History of the Plague: An Ancient Pandemic for the Age of COVID-19'. *Am J Med*. Feb 2021, 134(2):176-181.

Goldberg, Jeffrey. 'Sammy the Bull Explains How the Mob Got Made.' *New York Times Magazine*, 2 January 2000.

Google. (n.d.). [The Godfather 3 shooting scene] www.google.com/maps

Gordan, L. (10 February 2023). 'Piana degli Albanesi: for its Albanian Heritage and the World's Best Cannoli'. *La Voce Di New York*. www.lavocedinewyork.com

Graham-Dixon, Andrew. Caravaggio: *A Life Sacred and Profane*. New York: W. W. Norton & Company, 2012.

Grand Hotel et des Palmes'. (n.d.). www.grandhotel-et-des-palmes.com/

Griggs, Yvonne. (March 2009). 'Humanity must perforce prey upon itself like monsters of the deep: *King Lear* and the Urban Gangster Movie'. *Adaptation*,1(2). 121 – 139.

Grinza, H., (6 December 2021). 'The Church Of St Maria Della Quercia. Viterbo ArteCittà.' www.viterbo.artecitta.it

Gross, Terry. 'A Look Back At "The Godfather," With Mario Puzo And Francis Ford Coppola'. *NPR*, 8 March 2019.

Grutzner, Charles. 'Police in Sicily say U.S. mafia attended '57 parley'. *The New York Times*, 2 January 1968.

Hager, Emma. 'Hemmed In: Kay Adams and Her Changing Fashions'. *The Godfather Anatomy of a Film*, 2018.

Hariharan, Janani. 'Men of the House: Modes of Masculinity in "The Godfather"'. *The Godfather Anatomy of a Film*, 2018.

Harris, A. '"The Godfather" and the limitations of representation'. *NPR*, 6 November 2022.

Haskell, Molly. 'World of "The Godfather": No Place for Women.' *New York Times*, 23 March 1997.

Henner, Hess. *Mafia* and *Mafiosi: The Structure of Power*. Gaithersberg: Saxon House, 1973.

Hesse, M. 'All eyes turn to Sistine Chapel's chimney during papal conclave'. *Washington Post*, 18 May 2023.

History of Castello degli Schiavi. (n.d.). www.castellodeglischiavi.com

Hofmann, Paul. 'Italy Gets Tough with the Mafia'. *New York Times*, 13 November 1983.

Hooper, J. 'Mafia's boss may dress as bishop'. *The Guardian*, 4 March 2018.

Hooper, John. 'Calvi was murdered by the mafia, Italian experts rule'. *The Guardian*, 4 March 2018.

Hughes, Howard. (2007). 'Riding the crest of a crime wave'. *Cinema retro*. 3(7), 36-37.

Independent. 'In search of. . . The Godfather in Sicily' *The Independent*, 27 April 2003.

Infinite Dreams Publishing. (15 November 2020). 'The Godfather 1, 2 & 3 Director's Commentary with Francis Ford Coppola' [Video].

Italia.It. (24 January 2024). 'Why the Acireale Carnival is the most beautiful in Sicily.' www.italia.it

Jacobs, H. 'They bought houses in Italy for 1 euro — and are using them to give back to the community'. *Washington Post*, 18 November 2021.

Jellinek, Roger. 'Just Business, Not Personal'. *New York Times*, 4 March 1969.

Johnston, Bruce. 'Corleone, the name that divides Sicily's Godfather town'. *Daily Telegraph*, 27 November 2003.

Jones, Jenny M. *Annotated Godfather: The Complete Screenplay with Commentary on Every Scene, Interviews, and Little-Known Facts*. New York: Black Dog & Leventhal, 2007.

Joss-Bethlehem, E. (2 August 2017). 'Something unusual at Bar Turrisi in Castelmola, Sicily.' *The Museum Times*. www.themuseumtimes.com/

Kearney, S. (23 July 2018). 'Taormina: The British Legacy'. *Times of Sicily*. www.timesofsicily.com

Kirchgaessner, S. 'Restitution of a lost beauty: Caravaggio Nativity replica brought to Palermo'. *The Guardian*, 19 October 2022.

La granja cooperativa que combate la delincuencia: Stanford Social Innovation Review en Español del Tecnológico de Monterrey. (n.d.). www.ssires.tec.mx

La Licata, Francesco. 'The Grotesquely False Myth That The Mafia Doesn't Kill Children'. *La Stampa*, 20 March 2014.

Laganà,Saro. 'Savoca, nozze d'oro con Il Padrino: così Al pacino imparò a dire "bedda"'. *La Sicilia*, 21 January 2021.

Langdon, Helen. *Caravaggio: A Life*. New York: Farrar, Straus and Giroux, 1999.

Le mamme del Borgo Facebook. (n.d.). www.facebook.com/cucinamutticiana/

Lebo, Harlan. *The Godfather Legacy*. New York: Touchstone Books, 2005.

Lewis, Jim. 'Palermo Privata'. *The New York Times Style Magazine*. 23 March 2010.

Lewis, Norman. *The Honoured Society: The Sicilian Mafia Observed*. London: Eland, 1984.

Libera Terra Le terre libere dalle mafie. (n.d.). www.liberaterra.it

Lichtenstein, Grace. '"Godfather" Film Won't Mention Mafia'. *New York Times*, 20 March 1971.

Liggeri, Domenico. (1 July 2020). 'A Savoca (ME) c'è un Asino Parlante. . . opera di steel art di Ucchino'. StoriEnogastronomiche.it.

Longrigg, Claire. *Boss Of Bosses: How Bernardo Provenzano Saved the Mafia*. London: John Murray, 2008.

Macuk, D. (29 August 2023). 'What's the Difference? Osteria vs Trattoria vs Ristorante vs Enoteca'. www.chefdenise.com/

Maggio, T. *The Stone Boudoir: Travels Through the Hidden Villages of Sicily*. New York: Perseus Publishing, 2002.

Marchetti, Silvia. 'Cannolo: The Erotic Origins of Sicily's Top Pastry'. *CNN*, 13 May 2022.

Massimo Stracuzzi, (2022). 'Savoca, Stracuzzi e l'emozione dell'incontro con Francis Ford Coppola'. Interviewed by Sicra Press.

Mazza, S. 'A Messina, nel museo buono per farci un supermercato aleggia il fantasma di Scarpa.' *Giornale Dell'Architettura*, 22 June 2017.

Mercatanti, Leonardo. (October 2013). 'Etna and the Perception of Volcanic Risk.' *The Geographical Review* 103(4), 486-497.

Merlino, Rossella (2012). "Con il volere di Dio': Bernardo Provenzano and religious symbolic ritual'. *Modern Italy*. 17 (3): 365–381.

Mignone, Lisa. *The Republican Aventine and Rome's Social Order*. Ann Arbor: University of Michigan Press, 2016.

Milhaupt, Curtis J. and West, Mark D. (2000) 'The Dark Side of Private Ordering: An Institutional and Empirical Analysis of Organized Crime,' *University of Chicago Law Review*: 67(1), Article 2.

Mitzman, Dany. (28 June 2012). 'Italy weddings: The ultimate gastric challenge'. *BBC News*. www.bbc.com

Mondello C., Cardia L., Ventura Spagnolo E. (2019). 'Killing methods in Sicilian Mafia families'. *Medico-Legal Journal* 87(1):27-32.

Murphy, A. 'Film Review: The Godfather'. *Variety*, 07 March 1972.

Murray, William. 'Francis Ford Coppola: Playboy Interview.' *Playboy*, July 1975.

Nico. (25 October 2023). A guide to Favignana – the largest of the Egadi islands. www.wearepalermo.com

NPR Fresh Air. (1 January 2021). 'Francis Ford Coppola On Making "The Godfather"'.[AUDIO]. www.npr.org

O'Malley, Sean P. 'A Glimpse Inside the Vatican & Msgr. Robert Deeley's Guest Post'. Cardinal Sean's Blog, 28 September 2006. www.cardinalseansblog.org

Online, R. (n.d.). 'Identificati dopo 64 anni i resti di Rizzotto il sindacalista che combatteva la mafia di Liggio.' *Corriere Della Sera*. www.corriere.it

Palazzo Chiaromonte. (n.d.). www.musei.unipa.it

Parco Archeologico Di Naxos E Taormina. Regione Siciliana. (n.d.). *Regione Siciliana*. www.Parchiarcheologici.Regione.Sicilia.It

Parco Fluviale dell' Alcantara. (n.d.). 'Nucia da Motta, Traditional Agri-Foodstuffs'. www.parcoalcantara.it

Parco Trevelyan. (n.d.). www.comune.taormina.me.it

ParTASTE. (9 April 2015). 'Understanding the Italian menu - Authentic eats in Italy'. ParTASTE.com. www.partaste.com

Payton, Jack. 'The Godfather, Part III: Palermo prospers as world heroin capital amid non-stop Mafia wars' *UPI Archives*, 8 May 1983.

Penn, Stanley. 'Colombo's Crusade: Alleged Mafia Chief Runs Aggressive Drive Against Saying "Mafia."' *Wall Street Journal*, 23 March 1971.

Pileggi, Nicholas. 'How Hollywood Wooed and Won the Mafia.' *Los Angeles Times*, August 1971.

Pileggi, Nicholas. 'The Making of "The Godfather"—Sort of a Home Movie.' *New York Times Magazine*, 15 August 1971.

Pioli, Giampaolo. 'Castello Pennisi, Sicilian Filming Location of Godfather III, for Sale for €6 Million'. *La Voce di New York*. 28 April 2023.

Piombino-Mascali, Dario et al. (June 2015). 'Paleoradiology of the Savoca Mummies, Sicily, Italy (18th–19th Centuries AD).' *The Anatomical Record Special Issue: The Anatomy of a Mummy* 298(6): 988-1000.

Pittas, Artemis. 'In Sicily, "Godfather" Draws Mobs'. *Washington Post*, 17 March 1991.

Primi, Fiorello. 'Technology Helps Resilience in Villages'. *Borghi Magazine*, 7(85), January/February 2024.

Puzo, M., Coppola, F.F. (10 May 1989). *The Godfather: III First Draft*.

Puzo, M., Coppola, F.F. (24 September 1973). *The Godfather: II Second Draft*.

Puzo, M., Coppola, F.F. (8 November 1989). *The Godfather: III Third Draft*.

Puzo, Mario. *The Godfather Papers: and Other Confessions*. New York: G.P. Putnam's Sons, 1972.

Puzo, Mario. *The Godfather*. New York: G.P. Putnam's Sons, 1969.

Rascon, E. 'A guide to the Italian ritual of aperitivo.' *America Domani*, 16 October 2023.

Redazione. 'Castel Sant'Angelo exhibition on justice in Rome along four centuries.' (20 June 2023). www.finestresullarte.info

Regione Siciliana. (16 March 2022). 'Ex Stabilimento Florio della Tonnara di Favignana.' www.visitsicily.info

Reilly, Julie. 'Till Death Do Us Part': Michael's Marriage to Apollonia and the "Corleone" Way.' *The Godfather Anatomy of a Film*, 2018.

Reporter, Rome. 'Disgust in Rome at mafia don's glamour funeral complete with Godfather music'. *The Guardian*, 4 March 2018.

Robb, Peter. 'Family Business: A journalist links the histories of Sicily and the Mafia'. *The New York Times*. 7 January 2001.

Robb, Peter. *M, the Man Who Became Caravaggio*. London: Picador, 2001.

Robb, Peter. *Midnight in Sicily*. London: Picador, 2007.

RSA. (16 December 2020). 'Mozia, an ancient Phoenician city in the Stagnone reserve in Sicily.' www.sitiarcheologiciditalia.it

Rushin, Steve. *Life The Godfather*. New York: Life Books, 2019.

Salvatore Quasimodo biografia. (n.d.). www.web.archive.org

Saracino, Z. '"Santa Maria del Guato": storia delle Pescherie di Trieste.' *Trieste News*, 13 October 2018.

Sardell, Jason and Pavlov, Oleg V. and Saeed, Khalid, 'Economic Origins of the Mafia and Patronage System in Sicily' (8 July 2009). In the *Proceedings of the 27th International Conference of the System Dynamics Society*, Albuquerque, New Mexico, 26-29 July 2009.

Savoca. (2024).' L'Associazione de I Borghi Più Belli D'Italia'. www.borghipiubelliditalia.it

Schlesinger Jr., Arthur. 'The Godfather Plays on Our Secret Admiration for Men Who Get What They Want.' *Vogue*, May 1972.

Schneider, J., & Schneider, P. (2005). 'Mafia, Antimafia, and the Plural Cultures of Sicily.' *Current Anthropology*, 46(4), 501–520.

Sciascia, Leonardo. *Il Giorno della Civetta*. Milan: Adelphi, 2002.

Scurria, Antinino et al. (December 2019). 'Sicilian Cannoli of Enhanced Stability'. *Gen. Chem.* 2021, 7, 210014.

Seal, Mark. 'The Godfather Wars'. *Vanity Fair*, March 2009.

Seal, Mark. *Leave the Gun, Take the Cannoli: The Epic Story of the Making of the Godfather*. New York: Gallery Books, 2021.

Sear, Frank (1996). 'The theatre at Taormina, a new chronology'. Papers of the British School at Rome. 64: 41–79.

Segall, M., & Segall, M. (26 March 2019). 'The Cannoli and its rich history.' Cannoli Kitchen. www.cannolikitchen.com

Sentiero dei Saraceni: Taormina – Castelmola (n.d.). www.alltrails.com

Shakespeare, William. (n.d.). *The Winter's Tale* (Act III, Scene 1, Lines 1-3).

Shales, Tom. 'The Godfather' for TV: a shattering epic'. *Washington Post*, 12 November 1977.

Shanken, Marvin R. 'The Godfather Speaks'. *Cigar Aficionado*, September/October, 2003.

Simonsohn, Shlomo. 'Jewish Settlements (2)'. In Between Scylla and Charybdis 43(222–266). Brill, 01 January 2011.

Sky News. 'Godfather-Style funeral causes outrage in Rome'. *Sky News*, 21 August 2015.

Slow Food Foundation. (2 May 2019). 'Motta Camastra Walnut'. www.fondazioneslowfood.com

Smit, T. (31 March 2022). 'Weaving Connections: Sicilian silk in the medieval Mediterranean.' *Textile History*, 52(1–2), 5–22.

Smith, W. *Dictionary of Greek and Roman Geography*. London: Walton and Maberly, 1854.

SpottingHistory. (n.d.). 'Pentefur Castle, Savoca'. www.spottinghistory.com

Sragow, Michael. 'Godfatherhood'. *The New Yorker*, 16 March 1997.

Staff. (17 January 2023). 'Italian curiosities: Florence's backward clock'. Italian American bilingual news source. www.italoamericano.org

Staff. (17 January 2023). 'Tradition of the month: the cult of Sant'Antonio Abate'. Italian American Bilingual News Source. www.italoamericano.org

Stanford University. "You've got to find what you love,' Jobs says'. *Stanford News*, 24 August 2022.

Steele, Gregg. 'On Location with The Godfather; A Discussion with Gordon Willis'. *American Cinematographer*, 24 February 2020.

Stefano, George de. *An Offer We Can't Refuse: The Mafia in the Mind of America*. New York: Farrar, Straus and Giroux, 2007.

Sterritt, D. 'An offer Hollywood can't refuse'. *The Christian Science Monitor*, 4 March 2005.

Stille, A. *Excellent Cadavers: The Mafia and the Death of the First Italian Republic*. New York: Vintage Books, 1996.

Taormina Film Fest. (n.d). Taormina Film Fest. www.taorminafilmfestival.com

The Economist. 'Trends in extortion payments by companies to Italy's Mafia'. *The Economist*, 14 June 2018.

The Godfather Collection Highlights. (n.d.). Academy of Motion Picture Arts and Sciences. www.oscars.org/collection-highlights/godfather

The Morton Arboretum. (24 March 2023). 'Black Walnut toxicity'. www.mortonarb.org

'The Mummies of Palermo in the Capuchin Crypt.' (n.d.). www.bnbdolcevita.com

The Nobel Prize in Literature 1959. (n.d.). NobelPrize.org. www.nobelprize.org

'The recovery of the Augustinian convent of Forza d'Agrò has been financed.' *Gazzetta Ionica*. 25 June 2022.

Theft of Caravaggio's Nativity with San Lorenzo and San Francesco. (5 January 2021). Federal Bureau of Investigation. www.fbi.gov

Thomas, Bob. 'Simonetta Stefanelli, Untouched by Her Fame.' *Associated Press*, 11 May 1972.

Thomson, David. 'Michael Corleone, Role Model'. *Esquire*, 1 March 1997.

Thonhauser, A. 'The History & Requirements of the Swiss Guard: the Oldest Standing Army.' (n.d.). www.ewtnvatican.com

Tim Shawcross, Martin Young. *Men of Honour: The Confessions of Tommaso Buscetta*. New York: Collins, 1987.

Tondo, L. 'Corleone: the Sicilian town trying to break free of its mobster past'. *The Guardian*, 19 May 2023.

Tondo, L. 'Theft of Caravaggio in Sicily still shrouded in mystery 50 years on'. *The Guardian*, 19 October 2022.

Triolo, Mario. (January 2012). 'Visita a Forza D'Agro' (Messina) descrizione breve.' www.forzadagro.net/

UNESCO – 'Opera dei Pupi, Sicilian puppet theatre'. (n.d.). www.ich.unesco.org

UNESCO World Heritage Centre. (n.d.). Vatican City. www.whc.unesco.org

UNIMA. (10 May 2016). 'PUPI World Encyclopedia of Puppetry Arts'. *World Encyclopedia of Puppetry Arts*. www.wepa.unima.org

UPI. 'Sicily Gets Hollywood Version of The Godfather'. *The New York Times*, 12 October 1972.

Vaticanoadmin. (30 April 2020). La scala del Bramante ai Musei Vaticani. Musei Vaticani. www.musei-vaticani.it

Verdi, G., & Solera, T. *Attila: a lyric drama in a prologue and three acts*. New York, Edwin F. Kalmus.

Villa La Limonaia. (18 January 2024). Villa La Limonaia: location per matrimoni e eventi a Catania.

Virgil. *The Aeneid* (A.S. Kline Trans.). Roman Roads Media.

Vivant Denon, D. *Travels in Upper and Lower Egypt, During the Campaigns of General Bonaparte*. Translated from the French. To which is prefixed, An Historical Account of the Invasion of Egypt by the French. London: J. Cundee for B. Crosby and Co., 1802.

Viviano, Frank. *Blood Washes Blood: A True Story of Love, Murder, and Redemption Under the Sicilian Sun*. New York: Washington Square Press, 2002.

VOA. 'Seized mafia land put to good use by Sicilian farmers.' *Voice of America*, 29 October 2009.

Welsh, James M. et al., *The Francis Ford Coppola Encyclopedia*. Maryland: Scarecrow Press, 2010.

Whitaker, Joseph. 'The birds of Tunisia; being a history of the birds found in the regency of Tunis.' Internet Archive. (1905). www.archive.org

Wierzbicka, P. (3 September 2020). 'Le mamme del Borgo' in the village of Motta Camastra. www.sicilylifestyle.com

Wilde, Oscar. (16 April 1900). [A letter by Oscar Wilde from Sicily].

Willan, P. 'Lady Chatterley lover unmasked'. *The Guardian*. 20 September 2017.

Wright, Charles. 'A Godfather tour of Sicily? Now there's an offer you can't refuse: Fifty years after the movie was realeased [SIC] in cinemas, Mick Brown visits the filming locations across the island and searches for evidence of the Cosa Nostra in Palermo, the Mediterranean's most sensuous city'. *Daily Telegraph*, 12 March 2022.

Xuereb, N. (2017). 'The architectural and decorative character of Villa Farnese, Caprarola, within the wider context of the artistic patronage of the major patrician families of Rome.' *Suburban Villas*.

Yates, John. (1975). 'Godfather Saga'. *Journal of Popular Film*, 4(2), 157-163.

Zuckerman, Ira. *The Godfather Journal*. New York: Manor Books Inc., 1972.

Горюнов, B.C. (2016).' The Liberty Style: Italian Art Nouveau architecture.' MATEC Web of Conferences, 53, 02004.

INDEX

Acireale 76, 96-116
 Carnival 110-111
Addiopizzo 117, 130-131
Addiopizzo Travel 129-131, 164-165
Adopt-a-monument program 123
Adoration of the
 Shepherd (Caravaggio) 36
Aeneid 133
Agrotourism 66-68, 73
Alcantara Gorges 70
American dream 8, 138
Ancient Rome 136, 152, 158
Andolini, Antonio 100, 157
Andolini, Paolo 100
Andolini, Signora 96, 100
Anti-mafia resistance movement 117, 130-131, 165
Antico Caffè San Giorgio 89
Antico Canto Siciliano 23
Antipasti 74
Antonello de Messina 36
Apalachin summit 107
Aperitivo 145-146
Apollonia 6, 16-18, 22-23, 27-28, 46, 77, 82-86, 124
Arancina al ragu, 131
Arancine 109
Arancini 46, 73, 109-110, 113
Archbishop Gilday 141-142, 147, 156
Art heist 128

Art Nouveau Liberty style 87-88
Atlantic City Commission meeting 105
Attorney General John H. Mitchell 11
Autobiography, Puzo 8

Bagheria 87-88, 112, 131-132
Banco Ambrosiano 147
Bar Eden 46
Bar Turrisi 89-90
Bar Vitelli 6, 8, 16-20, 23, 27, 29, 36
Baron of Santa Lucia, Franco Platania 68, 80-81, 86
Baron Pennisi, Gianni 108-109
Baruni 110
Basile, Stefano 43
Basilica of Santa Maria del Popolo 149
Bastiat, Frédéric 139
Battaglia, Letizia 162
Belle Epoque Grand Hotel et des Palmes 125-127
Belmond Villa Sant'Andrea 76
Belvedere staircase 142
Bernie the Tractor 163, 165
Bifora Quattrocentesca 36
Biga Genio e Farina Restaurant 120
Billards 120-121, 123
Blandano, Vincenzo 89
Bonanno, Joe 125
Borgo 16
Borsellino, Paolo 116-117, 160, 162-163

Bridge of Seven Arches 68-69
Buscetta, Tommaso 125

Cadaveri eccellenti 160
Calandra, Enrico 65
Calo (Michael's bodyguard) 17, 66-67, 77, 108
Caltanissetta 127
Calvary Hill 36
Cannoli 75, 127-128
Cannoli, chocolate inside, 127
Carabinieri 125, 160
Caravaggio 36, 128, 149
Caravaggio's paintings in Rome 149-150
Cardinal Lamberto 132-133, 139-141, 145
Carlo (Connie's husband) 123-124
Carnevanimale 111
Carnival Museum 111
Carnival of Acireale 110-111
Carpano, Antonio Benedetto 146
Cars 2 46
Casa de il Padrino 56
Casamonica clan 150-151
Castello Degli Schiavi 76-87
Castello Pennisi di Floristella See also Castello Scammacca di Acireale
Castello Scammacca di Acireale See also Castello Pennisi di Floristella
Castelmola 89-90
Castle of Pentefur 31-32
Catacombe dei Cappuccini 29, 134
Cavalleria Rusticana 94, 118, 150
Chair of, Michael Corleone death, 77, 86
Chiaroscuro 36, 128
Chiesa di Sant'Orsola (Church of Saint Ursula) 132-133
Chiesa di San Michele 6, 32-34
Chiesa di St Nicolò 23-26

Chiesa di St Sebastiano 64
Chiesa di St Trinità 50-53
Chiesa, Carlo Alberto Dalla 162
Chimney smoke, Vatican 141-145
Church of S. Antonio Abate 48-50
Church of Santa Maria Annunziata e Assunta (Duomo) 40, 42-46
Church of Santa Maria Della Quercia 133, 140-141
Church of Santa Maria in Cielo Assunta 29-30
Church of St Louis of the French 150
Cicala, Vincenza 20
Cicero, 127
CIDMA Museum 162
Cinecittà Studios (Rome) 117, 150
Cinema Nazionale 125
Cloister of the Cistern 139-141
Coastal invasions 96
Communist Party of Sicily 68-70
Conclave, Papal 143, 145
Confession, Catholic 141
Confetti. See also, sugared almonds
Confiscated assets 163-165
Contarelli Chapel 150
Coppola, Francis Ford
  Family 119, 23
  Filming 8-13, 19, 43, 46, 65-68, 76, 83, 96, 109, 112, 133, 136, 143, 149-150
  Script 9, 38, 57, 84-85, 91-92, 107, 123-124, 141, 149
  Statue of 20-21
Coppola, Sophia 119
Corleone train station
  (see Taormina-Giardini Naxos Railway Station)
Corleone, Carmela 40
Corleone, Connie 87, 120-124, 128

Corleone, Fredo 62, 123-124, 141
Corleone, Kay 10, 40, 44, 50-53, 56-57, 77, 83-88, 112, 120, 124, 141
Corleone, Mary 87, 117-120, 124
Corleone, Sicily 157-165
Corleone, (Anthony) Tony 53, 94, 117-118, 124
Corleonesi clan 158-159
Corso Umberto 76, 94
Cosa Nostra 11, 25, 116-117, 125, 128, 161
Cuccio, Marco 128
Cucina povera 74

D'Allura, Peppino 89
de Saliba, Antonello 55
DeNiro, Robert 81, 91-92
Desiccation seats 29, 60-61
Digestivi 75
Dioniso Di Morabito Andrea 26
Dolce 74
Don Altobello 91, 103, 105-107, 120, 124, 128
Don Ciccio
   Don Ciccio's Villa 96-101
   Nickname 102
Don Fanucci 54, 101, 131
Don Lucchessi 103-107
Don Lucchessi's house (See Villa La Limonaia)
Don Tommasino 66, 77, 85, 96, 132-133
Don Vito 42, 56-57, 66, 96, 98, 101, 103, 105, 111, 118, 126
Don Vito's birthplace 56-57
Driving, Apollonia 77, 84-85
Durazzesca Porta 50-51

Egadi Islands 134
Ellis Island 137-139
Enna 111

Erice 132
Etna, Mt 40, 70-73, 78, 89, 96, 107, 113-115
Euro houses 102
Evans, Robert 10, 43
excellent cadavers 160

Falcone, Giovanni 116-117, 160-163
Favignana 134
Feast of St. Lucia 26-27
Feast of St Trinity 55-56
Feudal system 78-80, 158
Filming locations, Acireale 96-115
   Castello Scammacca di Acireale 108-109
   Don Ciccio's Villa 96-102
   Sparagogna Train Station 111-112
   Villa Limonaia 103-106
Filming locations, Forza d'Agrò 38-65
   Casa de il Padrino 56-57
   Church of S. Antonio Abate 48-50
   Church of Santa Maria Annunziata e Assunta (Duomo) 40-46
   Piazza de Triad 50-53
   Via Belvedere 57-59
Filming locations, Mainland Italy 136-156
   Chiostro of Santa Maria Della Quercia, Viterbo 139-141
   Il Grande Mercato Ittico all'Ingrosso (Wholesale Fish Market), Trieste 137-138
   Palazzo Farnese (Caprarola), Viterbo 141-145
   Ponte Vittorio Emanuele II, Rome 146-148
   Vatican City, Rome 148-150
Filming locations, Motta Camastra 65-75
   Bridge of Seven Arches 68-70
   Village longshot 65-68

Filming Locations, New York City
   Little Italy, 9, 12, 54, 101
   Long Island 11
   Staten Island 11
Filming locations, Palermo 116-135
   Chiesa di Sant'Orsola (Church of Saint Ursula), 132-133
   Teatro Massimo 117-119
   Temple of Segesta 131-132
   Villa Malfitano Whitaker 120-124
Filming locations, Savoca 15-37
   Bar Vitelli 16-20
   Church of San Nicolò 23-27
   Wedding Walk 27-28
Filming locations, Taormina 76-95
   Castello Degli Schiavi 77-87
   Strada Provinciale 89-91
   Taormina-Giardini Naxos Railway Station 87-88
Fiumefreddo di Sicilia 77
Five Families, meeting of 126
Florio Tuna Factory Museum 134
Flower floats 110
Fratricide 62, 124
French Connection 125, 159
Funivia dell'Etna 113-114

Gaetano Porcasi 165
Gaipa, Corrado 80, 86
Galleria Borghese 150
Gambino, Carlo 159
Gangster genre 138
Gloeden, Wilhelm von 76
God's banker 146-147
Godfather culture 151
Godfather Notebook, The 57
Godfather premier in Sicily 119, 151
Godmothers 161

Grand Hotel et des Palmes, Palermo 125-127
Granita 18
Greco, Salvatore 'Little Bird' 125
Greek Temple of Segesta 131-132
Greek theatre of Taormina 93-94
Gregorietti, Salvatore 88

Heroin trade 125, 164
Honour code, mafia 100, 125

Il Grande Mercato Ittico all'Ingrosso 137
Immigration, Ellis Island 138-139
Inzerillo, Salvatore 'Totuccio' 159
Istituto per le Opere di Religione 149
Italian American Civil Rights League 11
Italic time 31

Jobs, Steve quote on death 135
Joseph Colombo Sr. 11

Keaton, Diane 12, 45, 56
Keinszig, Frederick 146-147

L'Antica Focacceria S. Francesco 131
L'Asino Parlante 22
La Casa del Cannolo 128
La Pietà 154
La Piovra 157
Lady Chatterley's Lover 89
Lady Trevelyan 94
Lake Tahoe 54, 112, 138
Lava, Mt Etna 70, 96, 114
Lawrence, DH 89
Le Mamme del Borgo 73
Lemons, Etna 107
Lena, Caravaggio muse 150
Libero Terra 131

Live nativity scene 63
Lombardo, Rosalia 135
Luciano, Lucky 125, 127, 158
Lupara 25

Madame Butterfly 120
Madonna and Child with St Anne 150
Madonna and the Serpent 150
Madonna del Carmine Church 89-91
Madonna of Loreto 150
Mafia
   art heist 128
   funerals 150-151
   lexicon 157
Magghia 63-64
Maggio, Theresa 157
Mancini, Vincent 53, 77, 103, 101, 106, 118, 124, 147
Marriage proposal, Michael to Apollonia 17
Mascali 76, 89
Mattanza 159
Maurizio de Lucia 161
Maxi Trial 160, 162-163
   Trial Documents 162
Mayor Nicolò Nicolosi 161
Mayor of Savoca 8
Medieval Synagogue 34
Messina, Province of 36, 65
Michael and Appolonia Corleone's wedding 6, 8, 16, 18, 22-28
Minniti, Mario 36
Monti Sicani 157
Moors statues 78
Morabito Andrea 26-27
Morvillo, Francesca 160
Mosca (henchman) 40, 48, 56, 103
Mosca de Montelpre (assassin) 89, 91, 118

Mother church of Savoca 29-30
Motya 121
Mt Etna Cable Car 113-114
Municipal Villa of Taormina 94
Museo Del Cinema 115
Museum of Legality 163 -165
Museum of the City of Savoca 28-29

Nativity with St. Francis and St. Lawrence 128-129
Neoclassical designs 18, 103, 117
Neri, Al 105, 141-142, 156
New York Times, The 11
Nicòtina family 32
Nino Ucchino 20-22
Norman Castle (Il Castello Normanno) 61-62

O'Neal, Ryan 43
Odeon (Taormina) 94-95
Omertà 159, 161, 163
Opera (show), 118
Oratory of St Lawrence 128
Oscar award 92
Otho 152-153

Pacino, Al 12, 19, 43, 45-46, 56, 76, 80, 82, 121
Palatine Chapel 134
Palazzo Caprarola 142-145
Palazzo dei Normanni 134
Palazzo Farnese 141-145, 154, 156
Palazzo Trimarchi 18
Palermitani 159
Palermo District Attorney 119
Palermo Mafia Summit, 1957, 125-126, 159
Palermo No Mafia Walking Tour 129-131

Paramount Pictures 10-11
Parsifal 127
Pasquale, Vincenzo borgo 20
Passo di Rigano family 159
Penis town 89
Pentangeli, Frank 151-153
Piana degli Albanesi 128
Piazza Duomo, Acireale 113
Piazza Fossia (Savoca) 16-23, 27, 36
Pizzeria Villa Zuccaro 88
Pizzini 164
Pizzo (extortion money) 129, 131
Placido Rizzotto cooperative 163
Pont Sant'Angelo 147-148
Ponte Vittorio Emanuele II 146-147
Primi 74
Provenzano, Bernardo 158, 163-165
Puppet shows 54
Putridarium 29-30, 60
Puzo, Mario 8-9, 13, 66, 84-85, 91, 107, 123-124

Quartarello 63
Quasimodo, Salvatore 38

Railway stations 87-88, 111-112
Raising of Lazarus (Caravaggio) 36-37
Red tuna fishing 134
Regional Museum of Messina (MUME) 36
Revenge
  Don Ciccio 96-101
  Inzerillo's son 159
  Mosca and Strollo 103
  Opera, in 118
  Vincent swears 120
Ricotta 74, 127-128
Riina, Giuseppe Salvatore 129, 158-164

Riina, Salvatore 'Totò' (see Riina, Giuseppe Salvatore)
Ristorante 'O Dammuseddu 58
Rocca Busambra 157
Roman history 151-153
Room of Messages (CIDMA) 162
Room of Pain, (CIDMA) 162
Roos, Fred 26
Ruddy, Albert S 10-11, 13
Russo, Giuseppe Genco 125

Saint Anthony 49
San Cataldo 68-69
San Luigi dei Francesi 150
Sant'Agostino, Basilica of 150
Sant'Agostino, Convent of 60-61
Santa Caterina Castle 134
Santa Maria del Guato 137
Savoca City Gate 34-35
Scala Elicoidale Momo (Bramante Staircase) 154-156
Scala Regia 142, 144
Scene analysis 7, 85, 100-101, 123-124, 138, 141
Sciascia, Leonardo 15
Scuba (Favignana) 134
Second Mafia War 159, 164
Secondi 74
Sentiero dei Saraceni 89
Shakespeare 38
Shakespearean tragedy 9
Sicilian Baroque 77, 99
Sicilian street food 131
Sicily Mummy Project 135
Silk production 96
Six second physicals 139
SP6 Highway 66
Spritzs 146

St Lucy's church 26
St Peter's Basilica 136, 146-148, 153
St Peter's Square 148
St Ursula's church 133
Staircase, spiral 142, 156
Staten Island 11
Stefanelli, Simonetta 82, 86
Strada provincial 78
Strollo 40, 48, 56, 102-103
Sugared almonds 22-23
Suicide 152
Swiss Guard 149

Taormina Film Festival 8, 94
Taormina-Giardini Naxos
    Railway Station (Stazione di
    Taormina-Giardini) 87-88
Teatro antico di Taormina 93-94
Teatro Massimo 117-120
Tempesta, Antonio 142, 145
The Conversion of Saint Paul
    (Caravaggio) 149
The Crucifixion of Saint
    Peter(Caravaggio) 149
Timpa 96
Trachoma 139
Trapani 131-134
Trattoria Anni 60
Trieste 137-138
Trinacria 92-93
Turiddu 118
Turrets, Feudal Estates 79

Upstate New York 13, 107, 126
Urzì, Saro 18

Varese, Giovanni
    Antonio Vanosino de 142
Vatican Bank 136, 147, 149
Vatican City 148-149, 153-154
Vatican Museum 156
Vegetarian offerings
    Palermo 131
    Taormina 88
Vendetta 46, 118, 163
Verdi, Giuseppe 136
Vermouth 146-146
Via Belvedere 57-58
Via Nazionale SS 185
Via S. Michele (Wedding Walk) 27-28
Vignola, Giacomo 142
Villa Limonaia 103-106
Villa Malfitano Whitaker 120-123
Vitelli, Signor 16-18, 46
Vitelli, Signora 20
Vitellius 152-153
Viterbo 133, 136, 139-145, 154
Volcano safety 114

Wagner, Robert 127
Walnut Festival 70-71
Walnut trees 73
Wedding night 82-84
Wedding Walk (see Via S. Michele)
Whitaker, Joseph 121
White Lotus Season 2, The 86-87, 120
Wholesale fish market (Trieste) 137
Wilde, Oscar 76, 116
World War II 69-70, 109, 116, 139

Zasa, Joey 105